Better Business by Phone

Better Business
by Phone

A Guide to Effective
Telebusiness Management

Valerie O'Dea

Ichor Business Books
An Imprint of Purdue University Press
West Lafayette, Indiana

First Ichor Business Book edition, 1999.

Published under license from Macmillan Press Ltd.,
Houndsmills, Basingstoke, Hampshire RG21 6XS.

This edition available only in the United States and Canada.

03   02   01   00   99   5   4   3   2   1

Library of Congress Cataloging-in-Publication Data
O'Dea, Valerie.
    Better business by phone : a guide to effective telebusiness
management / Valerie O'Dea.
        p.   cm.
    ISBN 1-55753-155-2 (pbk. : alk. paper)
    1. Telemarketing. 2. Telephone selling. I. Title.
HF5415.1265.O34 1999
658.8'4—dc21   99-39748
                                                   CIP

This book is dedicated to the memory of
Pauline Malindine
an excellent telebusiness trainer and sadly missed friend

Contents

List of Tables and Figures   xi

Preface   xii

Acknowledgments   xiv

PART 1   PRACTICAL TELEBUSINESS AND THE COMPANY PLAN

1   **Telebusiness and the Company Plan**   **3**
    What is telebusiness?   3
    Who should read this book?   3
    Marketing strategy   4
    Relationship, direct and database marketing   6
    Planning   6
    Telemarketing applications   8
    Investment   15
    Image   16
    Telemarketing strategy and plans   17
    What do we wish to monitor?   17
    Telemarketing and business processes   18

2   **Telebusiness and the Product or Service**   **20**
    Voice and data choices   20
    Software functions and features   22
    In-house or outsourced?   23
    Telemarketing from a database   24
    Telemarketing to the masses is 'old hat'   24
    Customer-loyalty and retention through telemarketing   25
    Brand building and telemarketing   26

3   **Telebusiness, the Sales Team and the Customer**   **27**
    Integration   27
    Relationship marketing   27
    The partnership approach   28
    Major account management   29
    Problem analysis and prevention   30
    Major account analysis   30

Partnership solutions 31
The customer's view 32
Our view of the partnership 33
Loyalty schemes 34
Data sources and management 34
Marketing database activities 36
Marketing database evaluation 38
Product life-cycle 39
Field sales needs 40
Information flow 43

PART II   PRACTICAL TELEBUSINESS AND THE MANAGEMENT PLAN

4   **Telemarketing or Telesales?**   **47**
Where do I start? 47
Call centres 48
Sales office automation 49
How does automation work? 50
CASM and ISM systems 51
The importance of integration 52
Project management 54
Telebusiness personnel 56

5   **Customer Service Policy and Internal Communication**   **58**
Customer service strategy 58
Total team integration 60
Management attitudes 61
Communication 66
Internal auditing 67
Empowerment 69
A simple solution 70
Teamwork 71
Loyalty through customer service 73
Understanding change 74
Quality issues 76

6   **Recruiting and Targeting Telebusiness Personnel**   **80**
Person specification 80
Lack of maturity? 81
Analysing the job and the person 82
Interviewing 84
Easy steps to good interviewing 89

Psychological testing 90
Performance standards 90
Performance review 92
Targeting 96
Incentive schemes 98

7 Managing and Training Telebusiness Personnel **101**
The role of the telebusiness manager 101
Motivation 101
Training and coaching 108
Short- and long-term training 114
Assessment criteria 115
Value-for-money training 118
How long should a call take? 119
Meetings 120
Time management 123
Understanding stress 126
Management information 128
Mentoring 129
Training schemes 129
Effective communication 130

PART III PRACTICAL TELEBUSINESS AND THE TELEMARKETEER

8 Reactive or Proactive? **135**
Inbound or outbound? 135
Auditing 136
Procedures 145
A marketing plan 148
Follow through 150

9 Image Projection and Telephone Etiquette **152**
Being an ambassador 152
Telephone service 153
A key to customer loyalty 156
Exhibitions 162
No thank you! 164
Not just a computer entry 164

10 Buying Behaviour **165**
The Pareto principle 165
Intangible factors 166
Business to business 167

Conditions and influences   168
Competitor analysis   170

11 Scripts and other things   **172**
To script or not to script?   173
Homeworking   173
Written communication   173
Debt collection   176

12 Telesales   **179**
How to sell   179
Buying criteria   180
Needs identification   182
A good listener   185
Selling solutions   186
Handling objections   188
'Closing'   193
Attitude   195
Negotiation   196

Annexes

A   *A paper on stress management and depression,* B. L. Corfield   199
B   *Standards and Regulations*   203
      The ISO 9000 standard   203
      White Paper presentation for DMA telephone marketing   205
      Regulations and regulatory bodies   210
C   *Example Forms*   211
D   *Case Studies*   224

Bibliography and Further Information   229

Index   233

List of Tables and Figures

TABLES

5.1   A manager's feelings and staff response   70
6.1   Performance standards   92

FIGURES

7.1   The motivation–hygiene theory   106
9.1   Three stages of counselling   158

Preface

It is predicted that by the year 2000, the UK Telebusiness market alone will be worth £10 billion and 2 million people will be working in it. Telebusiness is such a vast and growing area that you will find most books written about it tend to *specialise* in various aspects. For example, recent publications tend to concentrate upon the technological innovations and developments which allow us through computer integration to improve business by telephone. Others will cover specific marketing techniques related to telebusiness. These books, by specialisation and possibly assumption, exclude a breadth of knowledge and understanding in other areas. This book does not.

Whilst not claiming to be a specialised work, this book sets out to cover the breadth (and where possible the depth) of most subjects required to successfully introduce, manage and perform telebusiness.

Many related aspects of marketing including strategy, planning, database and relationship marketing are explored. Information technology resources are discussed through explanation of automation, telemarketing and innovations such as CTI (Computer Telephony Integration). Activities associated with the telephone including major account management, product life cycles, information flow and project management comprise the business management section of the book. People management material such as customer service, teamwork, motivation and recruitment are included with a dedicated section on telephone selling techniques for practitioners. Example forms, mentoring, stress management, buying behaviour, debt collection and case studies contribute to the breadth of subjects required for Total Telebusiness Management.

*   *   *

As a management consultant and sales trainer, most of the companies with whom I work at my entry point, aren't getting it right. Assisting these organisations to achieve bench mark productivity increases, staff with enhanced skills, and improved service levels has given me the opportunity to view both ends of a spectrum. Thus this book has been written from an experiential perspective and encompasses practical and realistic knowledge in all aspects of organisational and individual growth.

Much debate centres around Telecomms and IT convergence calling conventional management principles and techniques into question. Whilst I don't doubt the validity of progress, my work daily proves that **people** do not change. They hurt, aspire and excel in a variety of ways which as human emotions, remain unaffected by advances in technology. Voice processing techniques, number and line identification technologies, caller ID services, predictive dialling, fax processing, feature control and media conversion do save operator time, improve competitive advantage and enhance business processes. But they do not replace fundamental people management techniques which in turn are responsible for decreasing staff turnover, inspiring above average performance and creating loyal, motivated and customer orientated personnel.

You must decide for yourself whether improved systems and resources can replace people.

VALERIE O'DEA

Acknowledgments

My thanks go to Norman Hart who made the first approach, to Liz Robertson of Matrix Workstations and Phillipa Tozer of Market Solutions who were the only people to respond to my invitations, to Market Solutions again and Co Cam who provided the case studies, to B.L. Corfield for letting me print his paper, to John Strafford, Colin Grant, Fred Sheard, Neal McGuinness, Bill Woods and Ray Farmer who gave me confidence years ago, to all my clients and especially to the old pre-sales team at BT's Managed Network Services, Apsley, who let me view their projects.

Whilst writing this book, I developed a presently incurable and most distressing ear complaint called Tinnitus. I am grateful to Edward J.J. for his patience, sense of humour, knowledge, support and encouragement especially during the bad times.

VALERIE O'DEA

Part I

Practical Telebusiness and the Company Plan

1 Telebusiness and the Company Plan

WHAT IS TELEBUSINESS?

In its broadest sense, telebusiness is **any** activity connected with conducting business by telephone. Its closest synonym being telemarketing. Many people, however, do not fully understand telemarketing and still confuse it with old-fashioned telesales techniques. Those who have yet to get to grips with the entire sphere of marketing itself think telemarketing is merely a way of conducting research by phone!

To identify where telebusiness fits into the overall business picture, one could start with the following principles:

- Marketing orientated organisations uphold the view 'our business prefers to allow the customer to buy what he/she wants in preference to selling them the product we want them to buy'.
- Selling is just one of several marketing activities. Selling is part of marketing – not the other way around.
- The telephone can be used either proactively (outgoing calls) or reactively (incoming calls) or both.
- The telephone can be used either as a sales tool or a marketing tool – or both.
- The telephone can be used to identify and gain new customers or to service and sell more to existing customers.
- The telephone should be used in conjunction with other marketing tools. Most often, alongside some form of information contained on a database.

These principles will be expanded later in this book.

WHO SHOULD READ THIS BOOK?

The strategist, the manager and the practitioner all play a part in using the telephone as a business tool. Any size of organisation can benefit from telemarketing. Perhaps your company fits into one of these examples:

3

- Large organisations who have a dedicated telesales or telemarketing operation with an existing database of customer information held on computer, which is regularly analysed and updated. For example, a nationwide network of call centres wishing to ensure the system is fully utilised, best practice is in place and new developments not missed.
- Medium-sized companies who perform telesales or telemarketing activities, who have a computerised database of existing customers but don't perhaps analyse and fully exploit the information. For example, a company which wishes to further develop the use of the telephone within their overall marketing strategy.
- Small or start-up companies who perform little or no telemarketing or telesales activity and have little or no information stored regarding customers or prospects. For example, an organisation which wishes to ensure the appropriate steps are taken from the outset such that success will come early and little will need to be amended when expansion and growth is achieved.

Considering the telephone's established use as a commercial tool and its relative low costs, it is unsurprising that more and more organisations are turning to telebusiness in an attempt to improve their business. However, the outcome is not always successful – and we should first examine why.

MARKETING STRATEGY

Whilst inadequate training or resources are often initially blamed as the most apparent reason for failure, the more fundamental influences often originate from a more global lack of strategy, control and direction. As with any marketing project, the successful implementation and operation of telemarketing will only occur if it is part of the overall company plan. As telemarketing fits into only one aspect of the business plan, it is useful to examine some of the broader considerations first.

Because it can be argued that 'large' businesses have merely duplicated a successful idea which worked, the principles, information and suggestions contained in this book should apply across the board irrespective of the size of organisation in which the reader works. So irrespective of whether you are a director evaluating major product diversification or automation, a senior manager contemplating improved market-share, or an individual commencing a new company or department, it is important to decide upon a business *strategy* such that plans can then be made to ensure that the strategy will be achieved.

What attitude does your organisation have or plan to adopt towards marketing? This attitude will be a primary influencer of strategy. Most companies – by design or default – will have encompassed one of five main marketing philosophies – perhaps you will recognise your orientation:

1. *The Production Approach* which holds the belief that customers are only concerned with price and availability so that management must concentrate on improving production and distribution efficiency. This approach can be useful if there is excess demand for the product or when costs are high and must be reduced to increase demand, but is not singularly effective in achieving business success.

2. *The Product Concept* which believes simply that consumers want quality above all else. This value of quality is undisputed; however, focusing upon quality alone will not guarantee an increase in customers. The conventional four P's of marketing – product, price, promotion and place – are ignored in this concept.

3. *The Selling Concept* holds the belief that goods and services are sold and not bought, and directs all the organisational efforts towards stimulating interest in the product and disregarding the needs of the customer. This is still recognised in some double glazing and insurance companies, and whilst sometimes effective in securing an initial sale it significantly reduces the opportunity for valuable repeat business.

4. *The Marketing Concept* supports the view that successful business is achieved by identifying and satisfying buyers' needs. This concept provides the best clarification of the distinction between selling and marketing. Selling being preoccupation by the seller with his need to sell; marketing being the total focus upon customer requirements such that satisfying these will result in purchases being made without the need to sell.

5. *The Social Marketing Concept* challenges the marketing concept by questioning whether the perceived needs of the customer are really advantageous for their own or society's long-term interest. An example of this being smoking! Inclusion of consideration for society's long-term interests does have cost and profitability implications, but is nevertheless being adopted by many organisations exampled by those with a concern for environmental issues.

So the basic principles behind a strategy are:

- Long rather than short-term goals;
- Consideration of resource availability/allocation;
- Development of a vision or mission statement;
- Analysis of the environment;
- Marketing orientation/framework.

RELATIONSHIP, DIRECT AND DATABASE MARKETING

Relationship marketing involves the total organisation of business re-sources so as to maximise every encounter with a customer as part of a long-term plan to ensure *retention* of profits. The development of culture, products, service levels and resources along with people skills and attitudes are all geared to this goal. Telemarketing plays a major role in relationship marketing and other aspects of this are covered later in the book.

Direct marketing encompasses a series of creative communication activities. Specialised mailing techniques, elaborate copywriting and targeted visual aids each play a part in the purpose of personalised dialogue inside and outside of an organisation.

Database marketing is the compilation and development of information combined with effective analysis and decision-making which enables the 'data' to be used to competitive advantage – rather than merely being 'held on disk'.

In short, database marketing is a function of direct marketing with relationship marketing as the end goal. Telemarketing is involved with all three.

PLANNING

Modern day businesses do favour a marketing approach, and it is useful to look at this approach as summarised here:

'The management process responsible for identifying, anticipating and satisfying the customers' requirements, profitably.'
(The Chartered Institute of Marketing, UK)

Whilst primarily described as a management responsibility, a marketing orientated organisation creates the ethos and working practice which allows every member of the organisation to become involved in the process and this is heavily reflected in its approach to planning. Creating a team-orientated environment is not always easy but certainly worth working at.

The functions of a company (production, finance, marketing, information technology, distribution, personnel) supported via the two major resources of capital and labour carry different objectives, operate on different time scales, attract different types of people, regard money in different ways and are therefore prone to internal conflict. Preventing or addressing this conflict is mandatory in ensuring that plans are realistic and have received meaningful contributions from all necessary parties. Whilst on the surface a simple and obvious objective, my experience of working with hundreds of companies confirms that the many factors contributing to successful planning are either avoided, misunderstood or poorly addressed.

A further caution. A truly marketing orientated organisation will not just 'do' marketing functions such as telemarketing, advertising, promotion or product management as autonomous, expensive and ineffective activities. Adopting marketing as a business philosophy, with the entire company orientated towards the customer and each marketing activity complementing the other, ensures the synergistic result which total incorporation will bring.

Before the purpose or operation of any telebusiness or telemarketing activity can be decided, it is important for the company plan to be in place and for the marketing and business objectives of that plan to be defined. The following questions may assist you in determining your strategy and plans:

- What marketplaces do we aim to/currently serve?
- Who are our customers?
- How will/do we monitor changes in our customers' values, beliefs, wants and needs?
- What are our customers' current wants and needs?
- How have we targeted our existing customers?
- What are our strengths and weaknesses?
- What opportunities do we see in the future?
- What threats do we need to monitor?
- How well will/do we serve our customers?
- How well do our competitors serve the marketplace?

- How are we different to our competitors?
- How do we get our sales now?
- How well-known is the company?
- What are our existing and proposed marketing objectives, strategies and plans?
- What size is our market and what is its future potential?
- How well resourced are we? For example financially, personnel, information technology?
- How strong is our cash flow and credit control?
- What is our pricing policy?
- How technical is our product/service?
- How is short-term profit viewed in relation to long-term growth?
- How do we reconcile market positioning alongside profit margin?
- What is our direct sales effort when compared alongside our market development effort?
- Are we interested in deeper penetration of existing markets or the development of new markets?
- Is there conflict between profit goals and non profit related goals
- (e.g. workforce or social)?
- Are we orientated towards growth or stability?
- Are we operating in a riskless or high risk environment?
- Where is our product currently in its development or life-cycle?

TELEMARKETING APPLICATIONS

Telemarketing could be defined as 'all activities connected with anticipating, identifying and satisfying customers requirements, profitably, by anyone using the telephone'.

Assuming our expectations of telemarketing activity are realistically in line with the company, marketing or department plan, we can then move on and explore our preferred interpretation and application of the word.

Even political parties use a combination of direct and telemarketing to enhance their position! Many singular activities appear under the heading of telemarketing and here are some of them:

- Outgoing/outbound calls;
- Incoming/inbound calls;
- Surveying/researching;
- Qualifying prospects;
- Generating leads;

- Market intelligence;
- Compiling or cleaning databases;
- Collecting money;
- Recruitment;
- Special promotions;
- Customer service;
- Public relations and advertising;
- Gaining appointments;
- Following up on quotations/proposals;
- Support;
- Substitution;
- Test marketing;
- Dormant/lapsed accounts;
- New product launch;
- Exhibition/seminar invitation;
- Mail order/payment;
- Campaign penetration testing;
- Fund raising;
- Mailing list testing;
- Direct mail follow-up;
- Freephone;
- Cross selling.

The organisation's or department's goals and positioning are the starting point in identifying which of these applications are needed. The company size and available resources are then the main factors in deciding the volume of activity required in each instance. In deciding which ones are appropriate in your organisation, the following explanations may be of assistance.

Outgoing/Outbound Sales Calls

The terminology often used to describe the purpose of these calls is 'proactive', where the initiative and control is taken by the selling organisation. An activity which normally involves making order-taking telephone calls (often to a pre-agreed time schedule) to an existing and established customer base. Outgoing sales calls on a regular basis are more often performed by organisations selling a product or service which is bought on a 'repeat order' basis, for example consumables or upgrades. In larger organisations this is often performed by a dedicated individual or telesales team. The calls are sometimes made in addition to the selling efforts of an external sales force and sometimes as a replacement of field activity in the case of smaller accounts. Additionally, 'cold calling' in an attempt to secure at best an order or at least some level of interest is an additional outgoing sales call often made in situations where the company is attempting to increase its customer base or, in the case of a new company, to create its customer base.

Incoming/Inbound Sales Calls

The terminology used to describe the purpose of these calls is 'reactive' where the initiative is taken by the buying organisation, customer or consumer, with the selling organisation taking a more passive and responsive role. A primary example of this being where incoming order-taking telephone calls are received from an existing and established customer base. Reliance upon the buyer's decision to reorder is an important factor and, whilst being less costly than the outbound option, can dilute the opportunity to measure buying trends in the absence of a comprehensive monitoring system. Company size and sales-force liaison criteria exist in the same way as for outbound calling. Unsolicited enquiries would be dealt with under the heading of inbound calls as would response to any form of solicited call.

Surveying/Researching

Depending upon the purpose of the survey or research and whether it is an ongoing requirement or a 'one-off' necessity, this should be performed by either a dedicated individual or team. Surveys and research are more often conducted proactively by marketing department personnel in large organisations which have separate sales and marketing departments. Research can be performed for many reasons; for example customer satisfaction surveys, new product or service analysis and market trends. Professional sales personnel will use the telephone quite extensively to obtain information regarding potential (and even existing) customers so as to be appropriately informed prior to an appointment-making telephone call or face-to-face visit.

Qualifying Prospects

'Qualifying' in this context means ascertaining through a series of questions the probable level of budget, authority and interest possessed by the potential buyer. Usually this proactive, qualifying telephone call is conducted by a field sales representative wishing to determine whether a costly face-to-face visit to an inquirer is justified. Occasionally qualifying telephone calls are made by trained telesales personnel.

Market Intelligence

Not dissimilar to research and survey activity, but specifically geared towards competitor activity, market forces and changes. This important telephone role can be performed on a proactive project basis by a trained person as part of their job description or on an ongoing basis by a dedicated individual. Gaining market knowledge however would be a responsibility owned by every member of a customer focused organisation!

Compiling or Cleaning Databases

The exercise of database compilation normally occurs in three main instances:

1. A new company wishing to collate information with a view to contacting potential customers;
2. Any company with an established database wishing to collate prospective customer information within either a new product area or marketplace;
3. Any company wishing to transfer written records onto computer.

Database cleaning involves proactive telephone calls to establish whether information held within an existing database is still current and correct, for example names, job titles or fax numbers.

Dependent upon the time frames surrounding these exercises, database compilation and cleaning can be performed full-time by outsourcing, by temporary personnel or as a dedicated part-time element of an administrative or marketing assistant's job description.

Collecting Money

A less sophisticated way of describing the telephone aspects of credit control and cash management necessary in all organisations. This task is mostly performed proactively by one or more dedicated individuals within the accounts department, although in smaller companies it is often forgotten or given to someone to 'fit in when they have some spare time'. The rule which states 'If you can't do it right, don't do it at all' definitely applies here.

Many organisations are returning to the belief and practice of entrusting cash collection responsibilities to the field sales force. Some sales people are comfortable to discuss outstanding payments during a face-to-face sales call, whereas others apportion time to do this by telephone.

Recruiting

Undoubtedly a telemarketing function in that the placement and follow through of applicants can be performed more speedily reactively or proactively via the telephone. In instances where telephone use comprises a major part of the vacant position, interviewing by telephone is prudent. In circumstances where geographic or time factors are restrictive, the telephone interview is also appropriate.

In larger organistions this activity is performed by the personnel department, and in many others by the manager of the department in which the vacancy exists.

Special Promotions/Campaigns

Telephone calls highlighting attractive incentives, offers or discounts which can be performed either proactively (or in the instance where promotional material has been previously mailed) reactively. Special promotion calls are normally included as an integral part of the telesales job description and performed on an ongoing basis.

Customer Service

A term with many interpretations and meanings, customer service in a telephone context refers in many companies to the individual or team who deal – either as a dedicated responsibility or as part of another job description – with customer complaints. Additionally, customer service as applied to the telephone may mean dealing with client enquiries, technical queries, general information, delivery and stock processing, and indeed some companies use the term in preference to telesales to describe the personnel who take orders over the phone.

Public Relations and Advertising

Although considered to be a marketing luxury only for those organisations large enough to have the relevant budget, the telephone can play a substantial role in many of the lower-cost aspects of PR and advertising. A full-time role in larger organisations but equally productive if performed 'little and often' by smaller companies, proactive targeted PR calls can be extremely effective in producing worthwhile information, contacts and opportunities for exposure, as indeed a dedicated 'hotline' or individual will maximise the interest created by advertising.

Gaining Appointments

Often a follow-on from either qualifying or research telephone calls, the proactive telemarketing function of appointment-making is usually executed by field sales personnel. Equally often, a telesales operative will make appointments on behalf of the field sales representatives. A firm and confirmed appointment saves time and is a vital part of territory and business management. On occasions, appointments will be made by telephone as a follow-up to a roadshow, exhibition, advertisement or media exposure.

Following up on Quotations/Proposals

An important telemarketing function within the sales process. A proactive call to ascertain the decision, outcome or progress of a previously submitted written document outlining the seller's solutions (inclusive of price) to the buyer's difficulties or requirements. To maximise 'closing' opportunities and to allow for continuity, this call should be made by the sales representative who produced the quote/proposal; however in many companies, due to time restrictions or delegation of responsibility, the call is made by the telesales person. The conversion ratio of quotes/proposals to firm orders is worthwhile evaluating. It is surprisingly low in many companies and is usually due to the above point. It is recommended that this factor be taken into account when deciding who should perform the telephone follow-up calls.

Support

A non-specific function which should refer to the attitude of all individuals who have occasion to speak to customers and potential customers by telephone. As mentioned in the Customer Service section, some organisations dedicate a specific telephone help-desk for their external customers, and indeed others provide a support function to their own internal personnel working in the field (for example technicians, engineers or consultants).

As a Substitute

If an external field sales territory is temporarily uncovered, the telephone is an effective way of ensuring continuity.

Test Marketing

When a market area has been identified as having potential for the introduction of a product or service, the telephone is a cost-effective means of verifying this prediction.

Dormant/Lapsed Accounts

The fact that an individual or company once purchased is a strong basis upon which to make a telephone call to ascertain whether a relationship can be resurrected.

New Product Launch

To inform, invite or encourage a customer or potential customer towards purchase of a new product or service can be performed very effectively by telephone.

Invitations to Exhibitions/Seminars

Either alone or in conjunction with direct mail invitations, the telephone is a fast and inexpensive way of creating or confirming a delegate list.

Credit Cards/Mail Order

Many companies use the telephone as a way of taking payment for goods and services.

Testing Campaign Penetration

As suggested, rather than 'wait' for orders or enquiries to drop on the mat, the telephone can be used to ascertain the reaction to a particular promotion or campaign.

Follow-up to Direct Mail

As part of the phone/mail/phone approach to direct marketing activities, the telephone is a vital means of monitoring and gaining sales.

Freephone

Many organisations now provide a freephone service to encourage inbound customer calls.

Cross Selling

The telephone provides an opportunity to sell additional products and services to existing customers.

INVESTMENT

Whenever possible it is important to ensure that personnel, equipment and the environment are 'dedicated' so as to ensure effectiveness and success. This will naturally follow if the telemarketing function or functions have been selected in keeping with the company or department plans. In circumstances when this is not possible, for example in a small company, it is advisable to at least allow adequate time allocation for each activity. Unfortunately, many companies attempt to cut corners and tack a telemarketing activity onto an existing job function without thorough investigation into what is required to perform the task competently. The subsequent lack of resource provision, time allocation or training brings the result that one of the jobs may suffer or, at worst, neither are performed effectively.

An example of this which I meet regularly in my work is the management decision to instruct the customer service or order-processing department to commence telephone selling 'because sales have dropped'. The announcement of the decision appears in a memo 'Please attempt to find out what else we can sell the customers from our range' and more often sends the department into a state of panic. The individuals concerned are unable to sell, do not want to sell, have not been provided with any form of instruction in selling techniques, and are fearful of how they will be judged in their execution of this alien requirement. Result: demotivation, diluted customer service performance and even a possible decrease in sales.

IMAGE

With programmes such as customer service, customer retention and customer loyalty being increasingly introduced into organisational operation, it is vital to ensure that the objectives for telemarketing are correctly understood, planned and executed. Without this, the available contribution which telemarketing can make towards achieving quality goals will be lost. Alongside these preparatory cautions I would also offer my experience of working with organisations commencing telemarketing activity who have failed to consider the effects upon company image. As with many things, the introduction of telemarketing procedures can either damage or enhance the company image, depending upon what choices are made. Primarily, you must decide whether the function performed by telephone is as good if not a better way of achieving your objectives in preference to other forms of communication (for example face-to-face, written, computerisation, meeting, video conference) whilst still maintaining your image and reputation. We all know that an ill-trained and poorly motivated receptionist can lose us customers.

First consider what your image is within the marketplace. Is it traditional? Is it conservative? Perhaps it is innovative? Or maybe high quality? Is it modern? Are you known as pioneers? How has that image been formed? How much has it cost to create the image? If you aren't sure of your image, then why not perform some telephone research to find out?

Assuming you are happy with the company image and do not wish to make any changes, now ask the question, 'Does everyone in the organisation who has telephone contact with customers (a) know the image of the company in the marketplace, and (b) ensure the way in which they deal with customers is complementary to the image and that rectification steps are taken if necessary?'

Now refer to the list of applications, and having satisfied yourself that the selected activities are desirable and necessary from a business standpoint, carefully examine each one with your company image in mind and ask the questions:

'How does this activity affect our image?'
'How does this activity need to be performed so as to maintain and enhance our image?'
'What are the cost factors associated with this activity?'

If you are satisfied with your answers, it is time to proceed to the next stage of your telemarketing plans.

TELEMARKETING STRATEGY AND PLANS

As suggested, some telemarketing campaigns and activities much like many general marketing activities have been unsuccessful as they have been conducted with unrealistic expectations as 'stand-alone' functions, or have been operated without regard to the overall need for effective strategy and planning. This said, a growing number of organisations are still replacing their entire field sales function and in some cases their marketing function with telephone activity, proof that uses for the telephone are almost limitless and the term telemarketing far broader than many would consider. So, are you proposing to introduce telemarketing as an isolated activity which in reality amounts to no more than an attempt to sell more products over the phone? Or are the activities which you intend to use the telephone to achieve representative of a broader marketing strategy?

WHAT DO WE WISH TO MONITOR?

As monitoring is a primary activity within planning, it is necessary to consider not just what you are going to do with telemarketing but how the selected telemarketing activity can be evaluated. Most organisations have some form of IT use and strategy, and these days there are many Marketing and Sales Productivity (MSP) and automated telemarketing computer systems available. Although these systems do not compensate for a poor marketing strategy, sales force or product line, correctly implemented they should assist in achieving superior competitive advantage, impact and economy. Marketing and sales costs average 20–35 per cent of total corporate costs, thus telemarketing would be represented here. Automation contributes to the reduction of fixed and variable costs and assists management in equating actions with results.

Computerised telemarketing systems can be purchased independently but often form just one part of a total marketing, sales and management system. Often when company-wide automation is being considered, it is often the telemarketing function which is used as a test site, and as this is like putting the cart before the horse it is often an inappropriate selection.

Activities such as major account management, direct mail follow up, advertising response, call-logging, campaign management, competitor analysis, lead tracking, call planning, expense reporting, database marketing and management, journey planning, mailshot preparation, market analysis, research, forecasting, sales order processing, territory management, and of course pure telesales and telemarketing can all be supported and in many cases replaced with time-saving computerisation. MSP systems are available for every size of operation and can operate on single-user personal computers through to large-scale networks.

To evaluate your telemarketing automation options, the following considerations and questions may assist:

- Why do we want a system and what do we want it to do for us?
- How large is the project and what additions might need to be made to it?
- What resource is available to dedicate to the implementation and operation of the system?
- Is senior management fully behind the project?
- What training will be needed and is available?
- Can the system be added to or altered at a later date?
- What tasks will the system perform to enable us to 'add value' to what we offer the customer?
- What risks, benefits and budgeting systems are likely to influence the introduction of a system?
- How can we ensure that any pilot test will be fully realistic?
- How can we ensure that we account for any differences in roles, attitudes and responsibilities of those who will be selecting, possibly designing and operating the system?
- How will we overcome any resistance to the system among personnel?
- What do we need to monitor?

TELEMARKETING AND BUSINESS PROCESSES

Rather than just looking at the categories of technologies and packages available, it may also be useful to determine what business processes are in existence and to evaluate the effect of changes within these processes upon our purchasing requirements. This is especially important in larger size organisations where groups or networks of people need to access the same information, for example call centres. What support do large groups require? What barriers do managers face within a network environment and what are the implications for different types of organisation?

A telemarketing system should first and foremost be sufficiently flexible to accommodate change, whether caused by factors such as competitive markets, staff availability, the economic situation or political and global influencers.

Secondly, it should operate in a manner compatible with the managerial style within the organisation. For example, in an environment where there needs to be clear accountability, where specialist functions need to be maintained or where budgeting and accounting remain a management process, the hierarchical approach is normally found and favoured. If on the other hand the organisation is multi-disciplined, relies on spontaneous team activity or needs to work with diverse cultures, initiatives and responsibilities, a more responsive and reactive managerial approach is often found.

Multi-user Networks

Whichever style predominates, a multi-user telemarketing system should accommodate five primary needs, as outlined below with their accompanying advantages and possible disadvantages:

1. *Connectivity* – physical links between users, for example electronic mail; *advantage*: data can be shared speedily, *disadvantage*: resistance to change from traditional links such as fax and voicemail.
2. *Control* – able to provide management information, for example status reports and project tracking; *advantage*: provides opportunity for early changes and diagnostics, *disadvantage*: seen as increase in 'policing' and reduction in autonomy.
3. *Collaboration* – the possibility for sub-groups or project teams to work with information independently of the main group; *advantage*: can allow added value to the customer, encourages staff responsibility/creativity, *disadvantage*: some individuals feel devalued if required to share their knowledge, IT difficulties.
4. *Co-ordination* – of remote information (for example sales representatives with remote laptops to head-office processing); *advantage*: allowing external activity to be synchronised, speedily, with main stream activity, *disadvantage*: fear of changing familiar PC culture into a network, loss of independence.
5. *Change* – linking the data in a way which puts the customer at the centre of all transactions; *advantage*: competitive advantage, increase in customer response/loyalty, *disadvantage*: lack of marketing vision, no or poor accountability of network 'ownership'.

2 Telebusiness and the Product or Service

The standard sound signal analogue network of telephony has been enhanced and telephone lines are no longer used just to transmit voice information. Voice and data is increasingly being sent via ISDN (integrated services digital networks) which has improved the speed, security and cost of transmitting information. ISDN allows an organisation to link all of its national and global sites simultaneously.

To further understand the choices, plans and practices involved in successful telemarketing, it is important to evaluate the product or service involved. What is the unit value of your product? £10? £10 000? How frequently is it purchased? Weekly, annually or once only? How much technical understanding must the purchaser have? How many people are involved in deciding whether to purchase from you? How many people are involved with speaking to your customers by telephone? How many incoming calls do you receive? How much information must be exchanged or sent? If you deal in large volumes, then ISDN would be your logical choice.

The answer to these types of questions has a bearing on how appropriate it may be to use telemarketing as a tool to conduct business and gain sales. And also upon what type of computer software and functions you need to support the telemarketing activity. The combinations of voice, data and technology currently available are outlined below:

ACD (Automatic Call Distribution)

ACD systems are sophisticated switchboards which monitor incoming traffic and route calls automatically to waiting or specified agents. Call waiting is often denoted by a traffic light thus allowing telephone agents or operators to see the call situation at a glance and the entire system is backed up with a screen monitor providing real time information and performance analysis, for example: who answers the most calls? who is 'logged off' most frequently? who is the fastest at dealing with calls?

CTI (Computer Telephony Integration)

CTI is a technological innovation which allows what its name suggests; simultaneous and symbiotic use of previously captured data with new information defined during telephone calls. Different suppliers will claim different benefits, however the generic and technical advantages of CTI include:

- Transfer – not just putting a call through to a manager or another department, but transferring the computer screen pertaining to the customer or call *at the same time.*
- Call management information – individual telephone operator performance through call duration and result can be analysed.
- Marketing source – can be immediately recognised according to telephone number dialled.
- Computer dialled numbers – time saving and hands free.
- Information retrieval – from electronic, voice and fax mail systems.
- Queuing information – gives the caller the option to enter their telephone number and be called back.

DDI (Direct Dialling In)

Imagine an insurance company conducting a nationwide advertising campaign and inviting respondents to call a single freephone number. DDI – a network facility – can recognise the number, and thus the geographic area from which the call is being made, and re-directs the call to the appropriate local branch.

CLI (Call Line Identification)

Call line identification – another network facility – informs the telemarketeer of the number from which the caller has dialled and, if linked to a computer, caller details are automatically displayed on screen.

Predictive Dialling

Often used for cash collection, direct mail follow-up and other high volume calling, predictive diallers work through a list, dialling automatically and connecting only answered calls to the agent or operator – once again with screen details. Particularly useful when a telebusiness team are involved with both in-bound and out-bound calls, as monitoring allows adjustment. In other words, if a large amount of calls come in, the dialler immediately stops making outgoing calls. One of the main benefits of predictive diallers is the prevention and reduction of 'abandoned' incoming calls – vital in all situations but particularly in a customer service environment. Its forerunners, preview dialling (agent dialled) and power dialling (does not maximise the number of successful calls against the available agents), left the telephone operator with far less 'productive' time.

IVR (Interactive Voice Response)

IVR refers to systems which produce voice messages prompting callers to act in a particular way. Voice mail (individual ansaphones), 'your place in the queue', and new product information are examples of IVR use. IVR is computer linked and callers can request information from a database and even have it set to them by fax – without the need to speak to a human. Transfer to a 'live' operator is, however, an option in most IVR systems.

SOFTWARE FUNCTIONS AND FEATURES

Every package will have its own unique functions and your selection will depend upon what you want to be able to do, what type of product or service you are selling, and how you wish to manipulate the data you have or are acquiring. The primary purpose of most software features is to reduce or eliminate the time which would otherwise be spent performing these activities and calculations 'manually'. Some examples are:

- Account management;
- Sales process definition and tracking;
- Team selling and territory management;
- Notes attachments for opportunities, contacts, companies and so on;
- File attachment;
- Scheduling and diary management;
- Quotes and sales order generation;
- Forecasting;
- Currency conversions;
- Win/Loss analysis;
- Database synchronisation;
- Multiple addresses per organisation;
- Sales history and budgets by product for an organisation;
- Profiling by user-defined categories;
- Mail-merge letters or labels;

- Campaign promotion tracking and analysis;
- Lost and dead sale analysis;
- Quotes-to-order ratios;
- Weekly sales call sheets by activity type and time;
- Future call plans;
- Activity-based costing and analysis;
- Deduplication of names and addresses;
- Links to product specification sheets;
- Report and letter writer;
- Event administration;
- After-sales tracking, service and support;
- Scripts and sales prompts;
- Document image-processing and scanning;
- Update sales systems via the Internet;
- E-mail;
- Faxes.

IN-HOUSE OR OUTSOURCED?

It may be that whilst an important activity, the cost of performing your telebusiness functions in-house could be cost-prohibitive. For example, recruiting the calibre of personnel required may exceed the salary budget, or the space required to house a team may not be available. In that case, examination of available bureau services is worthwhile and the following questions may assist you in making a decision:

- How would outsourcing affect your marketing plans, your relationship marketing and customer service policies?
- Will you use telemarketing only for occasional promotions or for regular or daily transactions?
- Is activity constant or do you have peaks and troughs?
- What experience have you had in compiling a database or performing telemarketing previously?
- Do you have the resources available to operate the database, conduct the calls and analyse the data?
- Who will be responsible for the telemarketing and database activities?
- How would the telemarketing system integrate with other systems, for example accounts or stock control?
- What IT experience do you have in-house and how available is it?
- Have you run a telemarketing pilot already to prove its effectiveness?

TELEMARKETING FROM A DATABASE

Database marketing means storing and manipulating large amounts of data from different sources (for example purchases, enquiries, accounts and service) and presenting it in easy, accessible and meaningful formats (for example quantifiable values, positions, comparisons, threats or trends).

Effective database marketing means that the answers to the questions asked in the Planning section of Chapter 1 can be relied upon for accuracy. It also means selling effort can be more scientific, more precise and more cost-effective, through:

- Higher response rates;
- Improved conversion ratios;
- Up and cross-selling opportunities;
- Increased customer loyalty, retention and customer service;
- Better segmentation;
- Identification of habits and trends;
- Improved cost-effectiveness

And effective database marketing means understanding of customers, competitors and the marketplace can be improved. It can assist in identifying where our product or service stands in its life-cycle and market position.

CTI is the new innovation in database marketing. Telemarketing is the voice component of database marketing.

TELEMARKETING TO THE MASSES IS 'OLD HAT'

The modern-day revolution of a personalised service has created new marketing terms and activities such as 'marketing communications' and 'individualised marketing'. Simply put, people like to do business with organisations and companies who treat them as individuals, caring about their individual likes, dislikes, worries and problems. Customers don't want to be a mass entry on a computer or a prospect list. They want to be treated as individual human beings. If their problems are shared by other customers then so be it. We all still identify with groups. But recognition of an individual requirement or problem as being just that, is more in keeping with the emergence of individuality being increasingly craved by society in general.

Junk mail, 'cold' telephone selling and mass marketing were just three of the techniques used in the days when a company's aim was just to get the customer to buy the product which it sold. This impersonal, blanket approach was geared to suit the suppliers production capabilities not the problems of, or solutions required, by the purchaser. So, in telemarketing terms, the practices to be evaluated are:

1. How is your telephone call different to those being made by hundreds of competitors?
2. Are you operating in a niche market and what media communications are you competing with?
3. How much does your telemarketeer know about the individual they are about to speak to?
4. Is your telemarketing call designed to sell a product now or develop a long term relationship?
5. In what ways other than the traditional 'product, price, place and promotion' approach are you different to your competitors? How has the development of long term and individual customer relationships been built into your presentation?

The simple rule is to ensure that before a call is made or taken, the telephone operator, agent, telesales person or customer service representative knows – in all senses of the word – what differentiates the individual on the other end of the line from all other callers.

CUSTOMER-LOYALTY AND RETENTION THROUGH TELEMARKETING

The widely-known economic rule states that 'it costs five times more to gain a new customer than it does to retain an existing one', and whilst this is indisputable in terms of direct costs, it is amazing how many organisations still avoid the techniques and principles of retention marketing. Perhaps it is because retention marketing involves indirect costs in non-financial terms. For example, the 'cost' of making and implementing difficult decisions is discomfort. The 'cost' of training to improve attitudes is temporarily increased workloads. And the 'cost' of commencing a customer-loyalty programme is the lack of desire to adjust to changes in systems and procedures. Excuses such as 'it couldn't be done in the service industry' or 'with the unique features of our product, it wouldn't be suitable' abound. But this resistance amounts to little more than inertia and fear.

Telemarketing is the prime area for the techniques of customer-loyalty and retention programmes to be exploited. Humanised, two way communication opportunities occur far more by telephone than within field sales activity.

BRAND BUILDING AND TELEMARKETING

Conflict has long existed between organisational product managers and brand managers. The trend is moving towards a combination of these two with 'account stewardship' and 'category managers' (combining operations, branding and tactical marketing) becoming the new project management style job titles. Brand management is about the creation of unique product or service identity. One of the earliest examples of this being the Hoover. We didn't buy a vacuum cleaner but named them all by one brand. The promotion of a brand involves feelings and emotions. Trust, dialogue, frequency, ease of use, a sense of satisfaction and value are among many of the intangible tools which can be used to encourage brand loyalty. The broader application of these principles creates not just brand, but total customer loyalty.

Brand building and brand stewardship can be enhanced or devalued by telemarketing. Advertising and other forms of image projection can shape a brand but telemarketing coupled with database marketing can improve, develop and cement the company's relationship with the customer. Training people to understand what a brand stands for, what the characteristics of the brand are, and how telemarketeers need to sound to be consistent with what people would have witnessed in any advertising are all vitally important.

3 Telebusiness, the Sales Team and the Customer

INTEGRATION

This chapter addresses the many factors which combine to create the dilemma of successfully integrating the activities of external and internal sales functions so as to best serve the customer's needs. Although this is an achievable goal, many issues – and often entrenched views – need to be evaluated and addressed to create change and ensure success:

- Information about customers and prospects is often held in different places and filed in different ways. The results of this can cause time wastage, duplication of effort and an unprofessional image.
- External and internal sales teams are often targeted, incentivised and rewarded in completely different ways, which lead at best to rivalry and at worst to hostility and uncooperation.
- Skills and attitudes of field and internal sales teams can vary tremendously and give conflicting messages to the customer. Fundamental differences in recruitment criteria is often the cause of this difficulty.
- Differences in commercial awareness, perception of role importance and management approaches, all contribute to internal and external sales teams' beliefs about themselves.

RELATIONSHIP MARKETING

Integrating internal resources is vital if the customer is to be best served. Relationship marketing with the external customer can then successfully follow. In planning a relationship marketing strategy, an organisation needs to:

- identify customers' purchasing patterns,
- evaluate customers' responses to its marketing activities and communications,

27

- develop a strategy for special offers,
- select the media and marketing actions which are most effective,
- maintain the appropriate level and frequency of customer contact,
- measure the effectiveness of campaigns,
- develop a database which enables targeted approaches to be made,
- take into account the stages of product life-cycle and account development,
- change the role of the sales-force from focusing just upon new business,

and telemarketing, appropriately linked to database information and field sales activity, provides the opportunity to do this.

THE PARTNERSHIP APPROACH

After the Second World War, if a business could supply a product or service, they could automatically guarantee getting customers and orders. Things have obviously changed and buyers and decision-making units now have a plethora of choices in most industry sectors. At first it was changes in the product or service itself which set suppliers apart from their competitors. Nowadays it is the differences in their marketing and customer service policies which tend to provide competitive advantage. Relationship marketing requires a supplying organisation to provide a reason for the customer to repeatedly purchase and remain loyal.

Recent surveys conducted suggest that customers are seeking three primary provisions from their suppliers:

1. A partnership approach;
2. A consultative style of selling;
3. A problem-solving, solution-orientated attitude.

Thus, this must be displayed throughout every transaction, be it face-to-face, via technology or printed matter and of course over the telephone.

To assess opportunities for partnerships, how would you answer the following questions?

- What can you do to assist your customers to gain more business?
- What are your customers' major markets?
- What are their most important products?
- What are their new products and growth plans?
- What are their problem areas and success factors?
- Who are their main competitors?

In developing partnerships, it is important to know your customers' business as well as you know your own. An obvious place to start is with your existing major accounts.

MAJOR ACCOUNT MANAGEMENT

Because major accounts in most organisations contribute up to 80 per cent of the organisation's revenue, it is important that these accounts are treated with the respect they deserve. Often no attempt to plan for the future maintenance or development of these accounts is considered, and when they are lost it is too late.

In managing a major account it is useful to view the account as a whole business in itself given that it will often comprise many locations, divisions, departments and individuals. With the large volume of areas, resources and personnel to look after, it should naturally follow that major account management relies upon the assistance of all personnel within an organisation. Unfortunately many major accounts are lost due to the lone crusade of the major account manager. The first and most obvious groups of persons to assist field account managers are the internal telemarketing team.

However everyone, including the Chief Executive, should be prepared to be involved with the major account, and in an ideal world a full team will be dedicated. Often the team will consist of the salespeople or person directly responsible for the account, their own manager, representatives from marketing, design, production and customer service. Whilst it is also usual that these people will meet on a regular and prescheduled basis, it is more important that the individuals concerned are committed to the success of the account. This attitude towards commitment is influenced by many factors which include the relationship between management and operational people plus the views of management and the organisation towards major account management. Setting strategy is an important part of major account management and development, and as strategy is normally set by top-level and senior managers it is right and proper that they are involved and committed.

Additional members of a major account team should also include representatives from the account itself. A major benefit of this is that these individuals can be asked – on a regular basis – what their problems and requirements are. They also become part of devising the solution(s). These dialogues can be conducted quite appropriately by internal, telephone-based sales personnel.

PROBLEM ANALYSIS AND PREVENTION

Team review questions which can be asked to identify problems which may exist in a major account and prevent partnership opportunities are as follows:

- What inconsistencies exist in our account planning, for example geography or time?
- Do our strategies ever fail to make an impact, positively and categorically on our revenue and profit?
- Do we ever wonder about how reliable our system is for reviewing and measuring account plans?
- Do we ever lack the budget to do the job?
- Do we fully understand the major account or feel insecure in our position?

MAJOR ACCOUNT ANALYSIS

Time invested in analysis and planning will pay off in improved retention and profitability of your accounts. It will also assist in reviewing partnership opportunities. To commence your analysis, categorise your information into:

- what you sell your customers, and
- trends in customers' businesses,

and access the information from:

- your own sales data (past, present and future),
- the accounts annual reports,
- the media, libraries, and
- insiders from the large account

Everyone involved in planning and analysing a major account should know how your company is currently positioned with the account, how the account itself is positioned in the business environment, and what issues and trends are likely to affect the way you and the customer work together. This applies especially to the telemarketeer. The following is a useful checklist for analysis:

1. What portion of the account are we selling to?

- Do we have enough information to set a strategy for this segment of the major account?
- How much do we know about the internal organisation of the account?
- What do we know about the industry of which this account is a part?
- Does this portion of the account have high priority in terms of our current position and future sales potential?
- How and when might we expand outside of this portion of the account in the future?

2. What exactly are we going to sell them?

- What have been our major sales victories in this account?
- What sales are in progress but still to be closed?
- What problems or concerns may exist (ours or the customer's) about these outstanding sales?
- What (if any) losses have we had to the competition?
- What are the current opportunities in the account?
- Are we trying to place too many different products or services with them?
- Have we been too narrow in the selection of products or services we sell to this account?
- Which other segments of our company should be involved in developing this business?
- What new opportunities might be developed within the account in the next few years?

3. What contribution can be made to the customer's business?

- Does our contribution deliver profit-orientated results to the customer?
- Does our contribution help the account increase its productivity, boost its sales or lower its costs?
- Does our contribution give added value from the customers perception?

PARTNERSHIP SOLUTIONS

Managing a major account effectively involves more than just assisting them by supplying products and services as solutions to their business problems and requirements. It involves seeking opportunities to provide bottom line assistance which may not be related to our product or service in any way. For example:

- One manufacturer was suffering major industrial relations problems. The company who supplied their industrial containers loaned their highly experienced personnel manager as a temporary negotiator with the manufacturing union.
- A shoe manufacturer experiencing severe absenteeism resulting from employee alcoholism problems was invited by the supplier of its leather dyes to observe their own employee assistance programme successfully in operation.

What additional assistance could you supply to your major accounts? Be sure you can assist in improving its sales to its customers, reduce its operating or other costs, raise its level of productivity or assist in solving its business problems.

THE CUSTOMER'S VIEW

Now answer the following questions to build a picture of the account's view of the situation:

- What were the accounts sales and profit figures for the past year?
- Is there an upward, constant or downward trend in these figures?
- What is the account's own competitive position in the market?
- Who and what are its major competitors?
- Has their market share grown or fallen?
- What major pressures exist for them in terms of existing and new rivals?
- What economic trends are affecting the account's industry as a whole?
- What is the account's purchasing policy?
- Is the account centralising, decentralising or changing its management structure in any way?
- What legislative or regulatory controls is the company facing?
- Is it part of a heavily or loosely controlled industry?
- What political factors may influence the account?
- How does the account view our industry's place in its business?
- What are the account's buying habits and preferences?

- What criteria does the account use when buying?
- How flexible are its specifications?
- Who makes or influences buying decisions?
- Have there been recent changes in the pattern of this account's purchasing?
- Is the volume of the account's purchasing in your industry rising, falling or holding steady?
- What percentage of this purchasing is made from our company?
- How does the account view us against our competitors in:

  - the level of business relationship?
  - the understanding of customer's business needs?
  - how well the product fits to the customer's needs?
  - the positioning in the customer's organisation?
  - the product/service reputation?
  - prices?
  - helpfulness to the customer?

- What are our competitors' chief advantages, as perceived by this account?
- What does this account need, now or in the future, that cannot be easily obtained from the competitor?
- What would it take for the customer to buy from us what he or she now buys from the competition?
- In what areas of the customer's organisation is such a change of purchasing policy likely to happen?
- In order for it to happen, must the policy be changed at a higher level of the organisation than the one where we are currently positioned?

OUR VIEW OF THE PARTNERSHIP

To further build the situation analysis, answer the following questions from your own knowledge of the account:

- How well is the account performing in its own market?
- Does the account's own growth pattern give us a sales advantage?
- How much does the account seek our advice as opposed to just doing business with us?
- How much do we enjoy doing business with this account?

- Would we take a prospect or new customer into the account's offices to show off the partnership – or not!?
- Has the account bought more – or less – from us recently?
- What is our market share with this account?
- How does our market share compare to our competitors' shares?
- If the account is a growing company, have our orders grown along with it?
- Does the account treat us well as a supplier?

LOYALTY SCHEMES

Customers will change suppliers if they experience poor product quality; however, they are far more likely to defect if they experience poor service – indifference, bad attitudes or unresolved complaints. Companies which fail to analyse (and then effectively resolve) the cause of problems and lost customers cannot expect loyal customers.

Despite this, prior to the 1990s more focus and importance was placed upon how to attract customers to products and services rather than how to retain them. Loyal customers enable us to charge more money, reduce administration costs and marketing expense, attain more referrals and grow faster. Loyalty can be generated by habit, expectation of good service, money-off coupons, competitions, vouchers, guarantees, rewards, privileged service, memberships and cross-selling of other products. Analysis from data held detailing customers' reactions to various generators tells us which methods work and which don't.

We have all become familiar with loyalty schemes. We go to the supermarket or the petrol station and are given a card which enables us to accumulate points each time we return to purchase again. Many loyalty schemes can be effectively operated by telephone. A database can tell us whether a purchase has been or is being repeated. Data capture mechanisms on vouchers, for example, can provide information which can be used to plan future promotional offers.

DATA SOURCES AND MANAGEMENT

More information is stored in sales offices than is ever used! Data relating to products, the company, prices, customers, competitors and statistics can however be used to make sound business decisions, so how it is stored and the ease with which it can be accessed and evaluated is of paramount importance. To determine this, we start with four basic questions:

1. What information is/needs to be **held**?
2. How is/was the information **gathered**?
3. How accurately has or is the information being **maintained**?
4. How effectively has or is the information being **enhanced**?

We make the assumption that the cost of manual data collection, storage and management has been compared and favoured ill against the cost of some form of computerisation. Automation offers benefits not found easily with manual systems:

1. Feedback which enables long-term goals to be formed confidently, for example strategic policies for relationship investment and customer loyalty.
2. Automatic implementation of policies and procedures instead of relying upon individuals to remember and execute them, for example response time and format for complaint-letter responses.
3. Implementation and duplication of plans on a wider scale without the dilution which often accompanies the passing and dissemination of information via human communication.
4. Instant project and management information which allows prioritisation, access to point of need and capacity to see the bigger picture – not easily available with manual systems.
5. Empowerment of staff whereby support information can be used to aid the speed and effectiveness of separate departments and individuals, for example accounts information quickly available to a telesales operator during a live telephone call with a client.
6. Appraisal is accurate. The conversion of mass information into meaningful analysis allows specific review, accountability and action. For example the number of orders taken by one telesales operator, or the appropriate group of customers to mail regarding a new product line.

So important decisions for direct mail purposes such as which potential or existing customers to contact, how often, for what purpose and when, can be made once data has been interrogated. From this comes the steps of knowledge, decision, design, execution and measurement.

MARKETING DATABASE ACTIVITIES

Most information will be stored on some kind of database; thus, the day-to-day activities required to operate and manage a sales database are:

- Standardising data into codes or groups;
- Checking integrity of information;
- Monitoring duplications;
- Calculating summaries;
- Prompting follow-ups;
- Updating marketing programmes or special promotions;
- Recording mailings and calls and preventing duplication;
- Analysing response rates;
- Profiling customers and performances;
- 'Exporting' data onto disc for separate projects;
- Adding new fields or files.

Most computer software packages will complete much of the above for the telephone manager and operator thus saving them time.

There are two basic types of raw data: performance data relating to customer activity, behaviour and relationships; and research data either directly from customers via forms and questionnaires, or indirectly from independent sources and outside lists. Basic computer database fields required for data entry relating to customer information include:

- Customer name/address/telephone number;
- Contact/title;
- Credit rating;
- Sales/year to date;
- Gross profit year to date/percentage;
- Date last ordered;
- Products or services ordered;
- Lead source;
- Sales/telephone representative;
- Territory/category;
- Company size/no. of employees/revenue;
- Industry type;
- Capital and assets;
- Purchasing strategy.

However the list and permutations are vast, depending on what the data are to be used for. Also some information will be fixed (for example the company name) whereas some will be constantly updated and changing (for example last order value).

Additional information which might be gained, stored and retrieved for analysis is likely to include:

- Tips on new or different sales approaches;
- Production information about new applications, cautions, faults, developments and modifications;
- Price amendments, discount changes, credit restrictions, special promotional prices;
- Promotional information regarding national or local media activity;
- Company information including personnel changes, meetings, training schedules, procedure or address changes, new branches or expansion;
- Competitor movements such as new products or offices;
- Figures, ratios, stock levels, trends, exchange rates, estimates and forecasts;
- Appointments and enquiries.

Typically, information required for later use by the marketing department would be:

- *Campaigns* – for example, user, product, objective, results, scripts, 0800 number, cycle and costs.
- *Promotions* – for example, start date, response curve, suppliers, offer code, profit and segmentation.
- *Group information* – for example, description of previous buyer, quantity mailed and ordered, cell code, customer value increase by average, personalisation fields.
- *Media details* – for example, description, circulation, cost, length.
- *Third parties* – for example, type, owner, product set, number of outlets, data restrictions, rules.
- *Satisfaction levels* – for example, returns, complaints, attainment of delivery schedules.
- *Internal information* – for example, salespeople, regions, products.

For new organisations or those wishing to increase the numbers of customers on their database, there are many external sources from which lists can be purchased. Here are just some of the business and domestic details which may be available:

- Shareholder names;
- Directors names;
- Research findings;
- Main product groups;
- Number of employees;
- Postcodes;
- Marital status;
- Credit cards held;
- Appliances owned;
- Cultural pursuits;
- Equity capital;
- Turnover.

Essentially, almost any information can be gathered in questionnaire format and searching the numerous list companies for the type of information you require is a worthwhile exercise.

MARKETING DATABASE EVALUATION

Data can be interrogated to determine what information is already contained within it – thus preventing duplication of effort or information with future collection effort. Known as a data audit, sufficiency, completeness, consistency, validation procedures, recency sources and frequency are all checked, sometimes using statistical values but always cross referencing, so as to

1. maintain good ideas,
2. expose poor practices,
3. ensure availability of information is not overlooked,
4. identify unusual values, and of course to
5. confirm the data is ready for knowledge analysis.

Alternatively, the data content can be evaluated by asking, 'what is required to support my sales and marketing decisions?' For example, a definition might be to know the number of customers purchasing a specific product. If fields are missing to provide this information, they can of course be added.

Quality checks should be conducted on an ongoing basis to monitor duplication, integrity, error and decay. The results of an effectively managed database internally are:

- empowered users able to target prospects more precisely and qualify more thoroughly,
- a team-based approach adopted by IT marketing, field and telesales personnel,
- improved forecasting and upgrading through better information, and
- better opportunities to promote internal communication,

not least because, with recent integration procedures, the target audience is no longer selected by the IT department and the mailing pack is used quite separately by the marketing department!

PRODUCT LIFE-CYCLE

All products and services have a life-cycle. The stages of the cycle are commonly referred to as *introduction, growth, maturity, saturation* and *decline.*

As customers continue to purchase a new product or service, their experience in buying also develops. As products mature, customers purchase less-differentiated products. As the customer changes, the benefits they seek change as well. This subtle aspect to purchasing is often the reason why a telesales person, experiencing what they believe to be a stable and long-term relationship with a customer, is surprised to find that instead of placing the regular order expected, the customer has bought elsewhere.

A useful way for telemarketeers to evaluate this customer behaviour is to categorise them as follows:

1. *The Immature All Rounder*: When a product is at the beginning of its life-cycle, most customers are inexperienced at buying and therefore often place a high degree of importance upon technical and applications-support more than price. Decision processes often take a long time and involve more than one person. The entire package will be purchased with heavy reliance upon the supplier. Any degree of risk will be unacceptable.
2. *The Mature Specialist*: Once a product has become better-known and buyers more confident in purchasing, the buying responsibility is often given to one individual. This person is more likely to consider standard specifications and will be more knowledgeable about performance and application. Less regard or reliance will be placed upon supplier support and guidance and more risks will be taken. Decisions will be based more on price and made more speedily.

However, product life-cycles and customer maturation do not always happen simultaneously. The best approaches to take are outlined in the following augmentation of the four possible combinations: Where are your products and customers within this matrix?

1. *Early product stages/the immature all rounder*: Concentrate upon account management through new technology and individual support programmes.
2. *Early product stages/the mature specialist*: Keep the decision-maker dependent upon you for developments in the product/service and system development.
3. *Later product stages/the immature all rounder*: Focus upon providing superior service but accept that customers perceive you have similar competitors.
4. *Later product stages/the mature specialist*: Ensure your price is competitive. Ensure you supply acceptable quality and availability. Concentrate on customer loyalty and retention programmes.

Marketing and sales strategy should be considered alongside the above, and the role and behaviour of salespeople is of paramount importance – including the telesales person.

FIELD SALES NEEDS

It is expensive to put a representative on the road if their face-to-face selling time is not optimum and maximised. From a telebusiness or sales office manager's point of view (as opposed to a field sales manager) there are certain control advantages in tasks which are completed in the sales office as opposed to the field:

1. Efficiency of client coverage. More customers can be spoken with in a day.
2. Control and reactivity is easier as personnel are normally in one place under one roof.
3. The cost of an internal salesperson is far less than a field salesperson.
4. Purchase patterns can be monitored centrally, and thus improvements in interdepartmental liaison and cost per call can be effected.

As there can sometimes be confusion and conflict of interest, the fields sales manager and sales office manager are jointly responsible for ensuring that cooperation, communication and teamwork exists between the two teams. Sales office personnel experience a different type of stress, workload and pressure to that experienced by field sales representatives. For example, the field sales representative spends a lot of time alone, has relatively little contact with the sales office, and despite spending little time face-to-face with customers is judged on the amount of calls conducted and the amount of profitable orders taken. Calling on the right people is very important. A decision must be made regarding who to see, how many people to see and how often these people are seen.

On an ongoing basis, measurement of effectiveness is calculated. Cost per call, costs-to-order value, and calls per order are the three main ratios evaluated by management. These figures were once calculated manually by field sales managers, then produced by the same manager on a computer spreadsheet, however more and more sales office managers are producing these figures. Teamwork is especially important as the production and sharing of this information can be viewed negatively by field sales personnel if not handled correctly.

To avoid this, many organisations pair internal and external sales-people together in mini-teams and, equally often, will target them jointly. Mutual appreciation then develops with respect for the support and level of input generated from the sales office. Appointment-making, providing information, assisting negotiations, order taking (if only during periods of holiday or sickness) and after-sales service are key areas in which the sales office assist the field sales force to spend more time with the right customers and ultimately be more successful.

Automation of sales force activities and procedures is one step being taken by many organisations to assist in achieving this. Interface with telesales and telemarketing activities is an additional method of field sales support. In fact, replacement of field activity with phone activity is the direction which many companies are taking, and this is often enabled again by automation.

What does a field salesperson have to know and do?

- Understand how the selling being performed fits into the sales plan;
- Know how the sales plan forms part of the marketing plan;
- Understand the strategy behind the marketing plan;
- Understand the customers' marketplace and problems;
- Identify new customers;
- Identify the criteria for new customers;
- Be fully conversant with the competition;
- Hold full product knowledge and understand where it is in its life-cycle;
- Negotiate in-house and develop account management teams where appropriate;

- Know where potential exists and target calls accordingly;
- Understand the value of an account to the company;
- Know and apply margins;
- Operate with full understanding of revenue and profitability targets;
- Reduce time spent on non-selling activity;
- Produce reports, proposals, letters, quotations, presentations;
- Follow-up at appropriate times;
- Use support literature effectively;
- Develop relationships;
- Maintain relationships;
- Prevent client defection;
- Contribute to effective marketing communications and promotions;
- Process orders;
- Deal with complaints;
- Evaluate credit position;
- Open new market channels;
- Organise local marketing support;
- Arrange agents and distributors;
- Update information systems;
- Liase with in-house departments;
- Attend exhibitions;
- Actions generated leads;
- Seek referrals;
- Plan and implement effective territory coverage.

By examining this list, one can see:

1. How many field sales activities are actually marketing activities;
2. Where time is spent away from face-to-face selling;
3. How telesales and telemarketing can assist or replace;
4. How computer automation saves time;
5. Why effective database management and analysis is important for success.

In some companies the above list is entirely completed by the field sales personnel. In some, face-to-face selling has been completely eliminated in favour of telephone and database integration, but in most the tasks are shared between the internal and external teams.

The sales office could be described as being at the centre of all communications. Frequent direct (and sometimes indirect) liaison with customers, new prospects, the sales force, finance, management, credit control, marketing, advertising, dispatch, production and the market-place itself (research) means the sales office is at the hub. When dealing with an incoming customer inquiry, some action will be required which will then be sent or communicated to another department or destination. Similarly, an incoming letter requires sales office action – be it a letter or telephone call – followed by the response back to the customer. Processing orders involves liaison between the customer and distribution, receipt of representatives' reports requires analysis and transfer to management and files. Sales communications requires collation of samples, drawings, estimates and schedules with transfer to customer, sales representative and management. The sales office workload is a daily management of small and large projects.

It is vital that sales office personnel have a full awareness of company aims, an understanding of the department functions, confidence in the company's products and services and full product knowledge which can be conveyed in an appropriate manner.

INFORMATION FLOW

In my experience of training and consultancy, the secret to success lies in improving human communications. Very often I will interview a director, a manager and a practitioner within an organisation. They will tell me completely different things about the same issue! And will complain bitterly about the lack of understanding from the others.

No matter how spectacular the product or service, how sophisticated the resources or how up-to-date the computer automation, unless individuals work in an atmosphere of team spirit, understanding, shared goals and effective communication, none of the knowledge outlined in this book will be of use.

In simple terms, it is the senior managers' and directors' responsibility to set a goal, mission and objectives – which are fully understandable and achievable – and to ensure middle and first line managers are able to communicate this to the practitioners. The atmosphere within the organisation should be such that any difficulties can be openly discussed and sent back up the hierarchy without fear of reprisal. Until effective communication is in existence throughout an organisation, it is unlikely that the external customer will experience the reality of relationship with the supplier which is mutually aspired.

Part II of this book examines more detailed issues associated with managing communication and telebusiness.

Part II

Practical Telebusiness and the Management Plan

4 Telemarketing or Telesales?

WHERE DO I START?

Academic marketeers will claim 'The aim of marketing is to make selling superfluous. The goal is to know and understand the customer so well that the product or service sells itself'. It would then follow that teleselling is redundant if telemarketing is accurately conducted. A client recently asked me the question, 'We are about to recruit a telesales person, what do I need to consider ?' The way I answered him introduces the question 'Telesales or Telemarketing'.

Several questions have to be answered before a simple answer can be given. Firstly, assuming the person being called has heard of your company, how well-known is your product? Far more resistance is likely to be experienced if the product is new. Do you want the person to receive incoming calls or make outgoing calls? The next question is what market research has been conducted about the needs of potential customers. What is the problem they are experiencing which your product provides the solution to? How individualised is this problem or how blanket across your targeted marketplace? . . . You have targeted a market haven't you? Are they existing or new customers? Do you know the job title of the decision-maker? Is it likely to be one person – in which case it is going to be easier to get to speak to them – or is the decision-maker likely to be a unit of individuals who share the purchasing decision and may include users and specifiers? Next, have you decided what level of commitment you expect to be gained from the telephone call? Do you want to gain a full order – which won't be possible if your product is complicated or technical in any way – or do you want an appointment for a field representative to visit to be the result? And how qualified an appointment do you require? How long do you want each call to last – do you want quality or quantity of calls? What costs are involved in taking this person on? . . .

Further, what marketing communications are in place to support the telephone call? Do you have product literature, case studies, samples,

47

media coverage, advertising and so on? Is there a database in place? What systems, procedures and automation is available to support their activities. How well will they be managed and motivated? How many hours is the person going to work? And what specification have you compiled regarding the ideal individual. Have they sufficient commercial and product awareness to conduct a professional conversation with an appointment as the outcome? But given that in a lot of calls, rejection and failure to speak with a decision-maker are likely to be the reality, has the person you are recruiting got sufficient tolerance to rejection and personality quality to persevere without giving up or becoming bored? And how will they be remunerated? A basic salary only, commission only or a combination?'

Telephone software suppliers will claim that automation allows more calls to be made per hour, which whilst encouraging, poses the question 'how does one ensure maintenance of quality dialogue through quantity of calls?' This is further explored in Chapter 7.

In summary, effective marketing produces inbound calls, enquiries, leads and orders. Outbound telephone selling is often only necessary if insufficient inbound calls are being received. What are you doing to create inbound calls? Or to ensure every outbound call is effective through adequate planning and research? The days of cold calling from a telephone directory are over. This hit-and-miss approach should not be necessary.

CALL CENTRES

Setting up and running a call centre (inbound or outbound telesales or telemarketing activity) is relatively inexpensive when compared to the cost of face-to-face selling and always involves the use of computer software. As previously mentioned, many companies are now replacing retail and field sales activity with call centres. The most recent examples being banks, building societies and insurance companies who now offer their products and services 'direct' by telephone. Call centres are normally operated by larger organisations, although with the decreasing cost of software and automation (can now be used on a desktop PC) the benefits will soon be within the budget of smaller companies.

Freephone numbers and 'direct response TV' are on the increase and enable a large amount of data to be captured from inbound calls. 'Interactive voice recognition' software can be incorporated (in several languages) – if desirable – to take information from a caller when all operators are engaged. Brochures are then sent out with software prompting the operator to follow up on a certain date.

Outbound operations form the majority of call centres at present. To prepare for an outbound campaign or promotion, information must first be accumulated, either from existing databases (regarding previous purchases and so on) or created from scratch. Often the call centre personnel will work from a script and use software which allows 'predictive dialling' (which calls the next number on the list and checks it is not a fax or unobtainable, thus saving time) and provides marketing and management information.

SALES OFFICE AUTOMATION

Why should an organisation automate/computerise a sales office? This question can be answered by looking at some of the benefits that can be brought:

1. Time is saved and more information is available quickly. Improved management effectiveness should result.
2. Cost versus performance ratios of computers prove they are economically beneficial in even the smallest office.
3. Revenue and profit opportunities afforded by diverse and improved marketing communications applications such as electronic mail, interactive voice response and fax or video on demand could not previously be exploited with manual systems.
4. Telephones, printers, PCs and fax machines can be integrated thus saving time, preventing duplication and improving communication, efficiency and image.
5. The ease with which previously costly 'added value' and support services can be made available to customers.
6. The accuracy and availability of information increasingly required to make strategic decisions rapidly is afforded by automation.
7. Sales office managers can offer both proactively and reactively a more meaningful, fast and economic 'service' to those with whom they interact.
8. Information technology offers the option to reduce both personnel and floorspace expenses

HOW DOES AUTOMATION WORK?

Automation involves the process of manipulating information through computerisation. 'Information' can be anything from engineering calculations, production diagrams to stock control; in the case of a sales office it is normally customer details held on a database.

To explain this, we can use three basic terms. *Requesting, responding* and *sending*. These terms imply the need to communicate between two or more people, departments or computers. This happens through a *network*.

There are two main forms of technology which allow information to be shared across a network: *file servers* and *client servers*.

- *File-server* technology normally describes one computer system which houses information from which other computers can only *request* information in an unchanged, basic format, for example the *response* might be a list. (The information can then be changed when it has arrived at the requesting computer and the new information returned to the file server in its altered format.)
- *Client-server* technology describes a computer from which other computers in addition to *requesting* sight of information, can ask for complex tasks/alterations/changes to be applied to the information prior to *responding*.

And, finally, *applications* (programmes) run on the above network computing technologies. The extent to which the full functionalities of the technology can be used depends upon the features and limitations of the application. Examples of application software in a sales environment could be *contact management groupware* packages and *sales automation systems*.

Both contact management groupware packages and sales automation systems can operate on either file-server or client-server technology, thus the requesting computer can make changes or ask for changes to be made to information. However, sales automation systems have two primary differences over contact management groupware packages:

1. These systems provide the additional function of allowing any computer not just to *respond* to *requests* but to take the initiative to *send* relevant, *real time* information to other systems before they think of requesting it !
2. If the information sent requires an action, the task is automatically generated within the receiving system.

These programmes store their information in *relational databases.* Such databases (as opposed to basic, flat databases) are normally operated when it is necessary to prevent duplication or to save space on the computer. Basic customer details will be held on one database and an increasing, moving and growing amount of information which applies to that customer is created on a separate database. The two databases are linked by common fields and the mechanics of linking the two fields together is known as 'the relationship' The separate databases may be housed on one computer although it is likely they may 'live' on separate computers. Relational databases may run only on a file server but normally require the features and flexibility offered by client-server technology.

CASM AND ISM SYSTEMS

Computerisation has given us new tools and jargon to describe the various business activities and processes performed by sales and marketing departments. Computer Aided Sales and Marketing (CASM) incorporates database, telemarketing and sales management systems.

The database system controls the overall relationship with the customer and provides information to enable research, profiling, campaign management, performance monitoring, decision-making and event triggering. The telemarketing system is used to enable data capture, distribute and link calls, produce scripts, integrate voice response and link to other software. The management system is designed to automate salesforce activity by reminders of follow-up, diary actions, letters, reports, forecasts, territory planning, lead monitoring and links to electronic mail and voice products.

Personal Information Manager (PIM) systems allow basic storage such as schedules, names and addresses. They are popular, time-saving and the retail price is not normally more than a few hundred pounds.

Contact Management Systems (CMS) are more sophisticated PIMs which allow detailed *categorisation* and targeted *search* facilities through the creation of additional fields and screens. Features additional to those found in PIMs are contact tracking, telesales scripting, word processing, mail and fax merge facilities, sales forecasting and management reporting. Networked contact management systems can be installed and operated independently of other systems within an organisation. Most packages can be purchased for less than £500.

Contact management-based groupware systems are designed to provide all the features of a contact management system *to a network of users*. Communications such as electronic mail and task delegation can then be *shared* not only within the sales and marketing operation but through all other functions and departments. Even field sales personnel using laptops or notebooks can communicate easily back to the office with these packages. Utilisation of the Internet and the World Wide Web through data transfer and multimedia presentations is an additional feature of many contact management groupware systems.

On the other hand, Integrated Sales and Marketing (ISM) – also known as a sales automation system – involves linking all of an organisation's systems via computer technology – client-server architectures which support relational databases. In other words, other databases and systems such as accounts or order processing will be linked to the contact management system and all information can be *changed* in line with real-time business transactions if required and not merely shared. The business implications of introducing a multi-user network were discussed in Chapter 1.

Linking directly to the earlier argument regarding human communications and internal information flow, this requires all departments to share and provide information to one another thus allowing the field or telesales person to 'log into the server' and obtain total information regarding the client with whom they are speaking.

THE IMPORTANCE OF INTEGRATION

Many organisations planning to purchase for the first time or to integrate their existing but different computer systems face a dilemma when evaluating what they require alongside that which is actually available from suppliers. The emerging gap can be viewed as five distinct needs:

1. *Deciding what needs to be done and measured* so as to ensure the system is business – not technology – driven. What is the business strategy? What factors are critical to achieving that strategy? What are the impacts for the use of technology? What sales and marketing aspects require improvement? *Performance measures* (for example lead/sales conversion rates, sales calls per day and average revenue per order), *processes* (for example changes needed, cost of changes and return on investment), and *cost measures* (cost per sales call, training costs and cost of sales person chasing processed orders) all combine to make an objective business case for automation. The system supplier cannot do this for you.

2. *Deciding the degree of change required and possible* – also known as re-engineering. This can be performed in three ways. One surrounds a package, thus working practices are redesigned to fit the package. The second is incremental in that processes are re-designed one at a time. The third approach uses a blank sheet of paper and requires completely new ways of doing things. A bespoke solution would need to be tailored in this situation and whilst costly, will bring the return of improved competitive edge through customer management. Skills and resources are affected in each of the three cases and the system supplier is yet again unlikely to be in a position to assist.

3. *Deciding the level of integration required and possible.* As described earlier, how much inter-communication is required by your users? Data transfer integration allows basic sharing of information, for example, the sales department can send brochures out to customers. Workflow integration allows a user to monitor and manage the activities of another user, for example when telesales are making appointments on behalf of field sales personnel. Thirdly, user interface integration allows different systems to co-exist within the same system, have the same or similar screen designs, sit on the same computer platform and allow users a single point of access to different applications. An example of single user interface is the field sales personnel needing to have fast access to different applications in order to respond to varying client requirements. Single packages purchased should thus use 'open' technologies and be capable of interfacing with other systems and the purchase of too much (wasted cost and effort) or too little (benefits not realised) integration at the outset integration purchase should be avoided. Supplier claims should be substantiated by internal or independent IT specialists.

4. *Deciding the level of customisation required.* A packaged solution brings benefits and is inexpensive when compared to bespoke, tailored systems. The cost of a packaged solution rises when the potential for some future customisation is built into it and managers must therefore decide how their exact requirements will be met within the range of customisation available. The answer to this lies in the degree of change decided upon, and as explored in point 2 above the degree of involvement by the end-users and operators, and the strategic business requirements as outlined in point 1.

5. *Deciding the degree of coverage* required from the system. The technology issues involved in increasing numbers of business units, individual users and countries is a key issue for expanding and large companies. The system must be able to cope with different languages,

currencies, marketing strategies, technical environments and communications systems. Managing new performance measures, organisational structures, company cultures, project management, training, development and communications will result from implementing the system. These skills are not normally provided by suppliers so if unavailable internally, the manager should seek a supplier who has partnerships with third-party consultants or systems integrators with the right experience.

PROJECT MANAGEMENT

Many organisations are favouring project management as the preferred route to implementing change or introducing new systems and procedures. Instead of one individual taking responsibility, a team is created, as in the example of the account management guidelines described in Chapter 3.

As with most activities, project management requires certain skills and techniques to be performed so as to ensure a successful outcome. For example, many projects fail because goals might be unclear, the method of achieving them unsure or the person leading them lacks the required business tools or personal resources to ensure completion.

In simple terms, if there is a gap between what is required and available to complete a project then it is unlikely to succeed. For example internally, the commitment needed by a telemarketing manager may not be supported at senior management level. Externally, what is necessary for a client organisation may not be possible for a supplier to provide.

Projects have three main **phases**:

1. Definition of problem/requirement, goals and objectives,
2. Solution creation, and
3. Implementation,

and typically break down to the following **stages**:

1. Initial study, which evaluates application and outcomes;
2. Feasibility study, which involves assessing, considering, evaluating and recommending objectives, cost/benefit justifications, outline proposals, effects, timings and implementation;
3. Report consideration by decision-makers;

4. Detailed investigation and analysis (involving sub-projects if required) which concludes with decisions regarding specific requirements. Measurement, methods, process and critical success factors and risks are identified at this stage;
5. Facility selection where appropriate, for example from suppliers;
6. Resource planning, for example equipment, personnel, training, finance;
7. Installation/implementation; and
8. Review.

Many of these stages are now available within computer software packages.

Depending upon the nature of the project various **assessment methods** may be used to gather information:

- Mind Mapping – using multi layered visual layouts of main and sub-factors (normally expressed as mere vertical lists) which allow unstructured brainstorming to occur without loss of control.
- Surveys – of customers, staff or policies, which unveil assumptions and the need for continuance or change.
- SWOT analysis – the much-relied-upon method of evaluating strengths, weaknesses, opportunities and threats.
- Fishbone or cause and effect analysis – discussions focused upon determining problem and opportunity evaluation. Often involves flowcharting.

Some of the main **techniques** of project management involve:

1. Managing people and relationships – addressing issues such as teamwork, conflict resolution, empowerment and senior management commitment.
2. Ensuring required levels of technical competence – by evaluating skills, change management opportunities and integration.
3. Maintaining the process – by holding meetings, ensuring plans are up to date and following through upon agreed actions.
4. Maintaining the broader perspective – analysing risk, identifying benefits, managing contracts, budgets and documentation.
5. Establishing goals and monitoring progress – by prioritisation, communicating impacts of change, clarifying expectations and addressing fears.

A typical example of project management would be the automation of a sales office.

TELEBUSINESS PERSONNEL

As with any organisational position or vacancy, it is important to compile clearly defined job and person specifications. Chapter 6 deals with these issues in detail, however this section explores the generic principles of the factors which combine to ensure an individual is successful in a tele-marketing or telesales role.

The knowledge, skill and attitude triangle is a good place to start. Knowledge covers issues such as:

- Understanding of marketing and sales;
- Total familiarity with role responsibilities;
- Specific understanding of role link to marketing and sales communications;
- Company and brand ambassador awareness;
- How to use any available software and database technology;
- Knowledge about the customer's business and marketplace;
- Knowledge of the sales process and buying behaviour;
- Whether or not script-aided, a full knowledge of the effect of voice and words;
- Familiarity with decision-making units and processes;
- Informed of call number, quality and duration requirements.

This can be imparted with training although the cost of learning curves should be compared against the 'cost' of recruiting an experienced individual who will command a higher salary or remuneration package from the outset.

Skills, as distinct from knowledge involve practical abilities displayed through underpinning comprehension, subsequent chosen vocabulary and the sound of the chosen words.

- Commercial awareness through selected sentences;
- Responsibility indicated via sentence construction;
- Continuity of advertising or marketing messages through complementary language;
- Speed and accuracy when manipulating database information;
- Correct and appropriate words reflecting an understanding of customers' business, marketplace, problems and individual concerns;
- Effective questioning and closing techniques when and where appropriate throughout dialogue;
- Call control ability;

- Proactive confidence – not just reactive passivity and information-giving;
- Compliance with standards, targets and objectives

Attitudes result from an amalgam of more complex issues and have a direct bearing upon an individuals ability to use knowledge skillfully. These factors can be internalised or inherent, or externalised and environmental.

- Personal upbringing, personality type, barriers and conditioning;
- Extroversion or introversion tendencies;
- Personal problems or difficulties;
- Intellectual capacity;
- Flexibility, adaptability, enthusiasm, interest, reactions to change;
- Level of motivation and reaction to motivation stimuli;
- Working environment and physical comfort levels;
- Opportunity to achieve and be recognised for achievement;
- Tenacity and ability to repeat tasks without becoming bored;
- Tolerance or intolerance to rejection;
- Levels of assertion, passivity or aggression;
- Liking for responsibility;
- Reactions to risk, success, innovation, new knowledge and incentive;
- Relationship difficulties.

Thus, the criteria required for the position of an inbound call centre handler, taking simple, repetitive, frequent requests for brochure information, is vastly different to that for an outbound telesales person required to proactively generate leads or appointments from a relatively 'cold' starting point. Successful planning and execution of interviews, training and resources will ensure square pegs will be found for square holes!

5 Customer Service Policy and Internal Communication

Customer care, customer service and customer relations are business practices which have been familiar for some time. However, the reality of customer experience in many instances suggests that a customer service policy is something to which numerous organisations still only aspire.

No doubt we've all had good and bad experiences as customers. In my work I am constantly aware of service, and two incidents stay distinctly with me. In a London restaurant I once complained about the lack of minced meat in a spaghetti bolognaise I had ordered. The waiter peered at my plate and said, 'It looks like meat to me. If you want more, order steak!' Needless to say, I made my dissatisfaction known to the owner and never ate in the restaurant again. On another occasion I had cause to return a product to Johnson & Johnson because it had caused a skin irritation. Their first response was to send me a letter of apology along with a voucher for ten times the amount of the original product cost. Pleased with this response, I was even more delighted one month later when a further voucher, this time with only the subtlety of a compliments slip, arrived in the post. I continue to buy their products and my satisfaction is borne out by the fact that I am printing the story. No doubt the posting of the second set of vouchers was triggered by a computer, however even with knowledge of this the attention to my personal experience was not devalued in any way.

CUSTOMER SERVICE STRATEGY

Poor customer service can be defined as 'the gap which exists between the customer's expectation and experience', and good customer service as 'exceeding the customer's expectations'.

Terms such as 'customer care' and 'customer service' can mean anything from another name for the reactive complaints department, through to a full-blown proactive policy of aims and behaviours which encourage retention through satisfaction.

Many organisations have now developed customer service strategies and charters. Government departments, hospitals, supermarkets and hotels, all place in writing the specific goals to which they aspire and publish proudly their near or over achievement of these quantifiable objectives. The Post Office standards include '. . . ensuring customers wait for less than five minutes to be served . . . and if we run out of forms, we'll post them to you free of charge'.

Meaningful customer service strategies will encompass most if not all of the following:

- Policy is in writing;
- Monitoring of customer service levels on a regular basis;
- Staff who are 'able' to get close to the customer;
- Build the strategy based on the customers' definition of service – not the company's;
- Empowered personnel, able to resolve complaints;
- Accessibility to the company is easy and unblocked;
- Seek to ensure win–win outcomes to a complaint;
- Use technology to improve services;
- Value the customer service role (career not just a job);
- Focus on customer retention and loyalty.

These issues should be set by the organisation and steered by management. They are not things which front-line practitioners can just automatically 'do'.

The first step in developing a customer service strategy is to identify your current service position. Data and information which will tell you what is important to your customers is paramount. Looking at yourself through the eyes of the customer, identifying why customers actually buy from you and knowing what is unique or distinct about your product or service is vital. The way to find this information is to communicate with your customers – in other words, ask them! Talk to the ones who have left you as well. What would it take to get them back? What was the attraction with the alternative they chose? What can you learn from your competitors so as to further evaluate your service position? How are they performing on what's important to the customer? Why do they win or lose orders? And how do you segment your customers? Segmenting the medical market into hospitals and GPs is not enough. Some GPs will want the cheapest generic drug whilst others will be interested in the brand leader. Are your customers' needs treated as grouped or individualised?

The second stage is to use this information to create and clarify the service vision of senior management and communicate this to employees and customers. A service vision is a statement about the future and of how the company wishes to be perceived by customers, and defines the purpose or mission of the organisation with respect to serving customers. It forces an answer to the question: which business are we in? It identifies the specific group or groups of customers you intend to serve, the needs which you intend to fulfill in terms of results to be produced for customers and is specific about what it takes to get and keep customers in your business.

For the vision to be effective, the organisation must have complementary and realistic processes, procedures and structures. This is the third step, making the strategy happen. It is the hardest step because it involves changes in attitudes and procedures and often requires a radical change from being company to customer-directed. Service standards must be identified for key activities, and employee performance should mirror customer needs. What can your organisation do to assist your employees to better serve the customer? What can be added or taken away? Do internal rules, regulations or politics get in the way and make it difficult for employees to serve the customer? How well-trained are your staff to serve the customer? How easy is it for the customer to complain and what information technology is in place to assist you and your employees to carry out your customer service strategy?

TOTAL TEAM INTEGRATION

Most corporate strategy statements never actually penetrate the ranks of management to touch the minds and imaginations of the employees doing the everyday work of the company. What customers think of your business will not be based on any well meaning or high sounding mission statements emanating from the board, but on their experience of how they are treated by first line employees. If your employees don't know what the strategy of the business is, or can't translate it into workable terms, the strategy will simply grind to oblivion somewhere in the offices of senior management.

(David Drennan, Special Professor of Management,
Nottingham University)

Use the following questions as a checklist to determine how well you communicate with your staff regarding key business messages:

1. I have explained to my staff the company's policy on quality and service to the customer and how it relates practically to our department;
2. I have agreed specific goals and performance benchmarks on quality and service with my staff;
3. . . . and we regularly measure and discuss progress and problems;
4. I frequently remind my staff in informal discussion why the customer must come first;
5. I often ask my staff for their perception of customers' needs and expectations;
6. I regularly and personally ask customers about their needs and satisfaction with our performance;
7. I set my staff a good example in the way I deal with external and internal customers;
8. I work in a team with my colleagues and boss to identify and remove obstacles to good service, which are not my sole responsibility (e.g. delays, discourtesies);
9. I make sure that the theme 'we are here to secure, satisfy and hold customers' runs through all training given to my staff;
10. Since I know our customers have choices, I study regularly the service performance of our main competitors.

MANAGEMENT ATTITUDES

In an ideal world a manager will give equal importance and attention to staff, productivity and customers. Personality often plays a big part in orientating a manager to being staff-focused to the detriment of business, or business-focused to the detriment of staff. The required balance is also affected when self-preservation becomes the most important factor. The aim of an organisation is to ensure an environment where systems and procedures protect the staff and customers from the negative effects of imbalanced management biases, orientations and attitudes.

Management attitudes to staff and customers is one of the most important factors in determining the success or failure of customer service strategies. As part of my consultancy activity I have encountered on numerous occasions negative attitudes and feelings which at best have caused conflict and delay, and at worst caused the required transformation or project to come to a grinding halt! The paralysing effect of feelings are typified in the following examples where my intervention as an external, safe, third-party assisted in resolving or exposing the problem:

Fear of challenging or standing up to senior managers

In an insurance organisation, the junior manager was keen, experienced and well in touch with what customers wanted in his sphere of the business. He was an excellent manager and knew about the day-to-day difficulties experienced by his staff. No system existed to enable the staff to target either existing or new customers, and the personnel had been recruited from a clerical background. The board and senior management demanded to see growth in his division and suggested that sales training was required to secure the increase. The manager knew that sales training was not the solution. A fundamental decision regarding the positioning of the division accompanied with a revamped job profile and recruitment policy was more appropriate. The sales training audit I performed highlighted this and the manager used the objectivity of my report to approach the board with his views and recommendations. His proposals were accepted and the training solution dropped. The problem had existed for two years prior to my visit and only the manager's fear of challenging and standing up to senior management had prevented them from knowing the facts. Time had been wasted because of how the manager felt.

Fear of losing power, status or control

A large retail furniture company operated with a central training department. In this organisation the value of training was not recognised and it was considered that 'failed managers' were sent to the training department. The training manager, however, was the head of a large department. Training was not viewed as a management tool, nor as part of the individual's or organisation's development, although it was mandatory for every member of personnel to receive a certain number of days training per year. The case for the internal customer did not form part of the organisation's ethos, and every department operated with the "so long as we're all right, who cares about their problems" attitude to one another. The training audit I performed highlighted these issues and brought them to the attention of senior management. Horrified, they rapidly embarked upon an internal PR programme which involved the addition of training to the list of responsibilities for each line manager. Whilst this succeeded in improving the value and view of training throughout the organisation, the training manager believed his department would become less important. His feelings of fear of losing power, status and control were so strong that he resigned.

Fear of conflict and hostility

During a telesales course, the telesales manager of a small motorparts company admitted to me that she was at the end of her tether with two of the telemarketing team members. They were regularly underperforming but being quite aggressive when counselled. The team were measured on a collective target and the other hardworking team members had repeatedly expressed the frustration of 'carrying' the two lesser performers. The manager had long since realised that a change to individual targets was both necessary and appropriate, however she admitted to being frightened of what she believed would be the negative reactions of the two under-achievers. She claimed to be 'no good at handling conflict'. Senior management were satisfied with the team result and were ignorant of the problem. They only stepped in to assist the manager in resolving the problem when I brought the issue to their attention. It was also suggested that the manager attend an assertiveness course as her fear of conflict was preventing her from implementing what everyone knew was the correct management action. Her fear of two people's aggressive reaction was stronger than her concerns for the business objectives and the motivation levels of the rest of the team.

Fear of retribution, exposure, change

A large telecommunications organisation requested me to audit the management team of their customer service department. The manager was newly promoted from another department and his strengths and experience lay elsewhere than in customer service practices. He held the view that bad attitudes among managers were causing demotivation and poor performance within the department. My investigations caused me to agree with him, but we disagreed about the reasons for the poor attitudes and the subsequent activity required to improve them. He felt that weakness, inability and poor decision-making were the sole cause, and that training would impart new knowledge required to improve skills. Training did help, but the poor attitudes were more reflective of inadequate, insufficient technology required to support the volume of incoming calls along with a lack of direction from previous management. The new manager was himself weak, unable, and poor at making decisions. Often, that which we criticise in others is what we wish we were better at ourselves! In eventually providing more direction and support to the management team, the department manager was rewarded by an improvement in their attitudes. This was not before he had to face and overcome his own fears of change (his own new areas of learning), retribution (the results if decisions he made backfired) and exposure (his own managerial weaknesses).

Unprepared to admit errors and mistakes

My brief with an electronic instrument company was to 'improve teamwork'. Productivity was down, and the senior manager with whom I spoke quite rightly indicated that encouraging his staff to work better as a team would result in improved output. The problem was, he did not see himself as part of the team or needing to be part of it. He listed the incompetencies of the staff and pointed out the various interpersonal relationship difficulties which existed. He was an excellent businessman himself with a thorough knowledge of the marketplace, the competition, the needs of the customer and the technical details of his own product. But he did not want to be part of a team himself nor could he comprehend the need to be. The teambuilding workshop proceeded nevertheless, and the personnel attending were totally preoccupied with their manager's refusal to be part of the team. Needless to say, he did not attend the workshop. His staff told me, 'if he would just once share some of the responsibility with us when things go wrong or admit when he has made a mistake, we would feel more motivated to work willingly and co-operatively for him'. When I relayed their request, he remained resolute but admitted his belief that if he remained outside the team he would not have to share responsibility for errors and mistakes. He felt safer on the outside. Many managers I meet feel this way, despite their obvious and ultimate responsibility for team productivity. I believe he was eventually replaced.

Uninformed as to what is required to manage effectively

The personnel manager of a large bank attended a conflict resolution workshop with his team. The interviews I conducted with his team prior to the workshop unveiled a vast amount of operational and day-to-day issues which were indicative of poor management. Personality clashes which affected workflow had remained unresolved, new systems available to the department were not being used or maximised, team members were being promoted to team leader without clear guidance of what was required or expected, and (internal) customer complaints about the department had increased. The manager claimed to be 'too busy' attending meetings and compiling board reports to involve himself in the day-to-day running of the department. This manifested in the team as democracy without guidance. During the workshop, the manager stated to his team, 'we have problems and I admit I don't know what to do to improve things'. The manager in the previous case would have learned from his openness and honesty, however his disclosures did little to earn the respect of the team or resolve the conflict. The workshop did assist with many of the conflict issues but the fundamental change necessary was in the manager understanding the importance of reprioritising his own workload.

Desire to appear cooperative and powerful

The managing director of a small printing company confided in me that his personal problems had prevented him from managing the direction of his company! He was happy to leave the responsibility for sales and service to his 'experienced' personnel who had formed deep and lasting relationships with customers, yet was equally happy to complain about their manipulative approach towards salary increases, working hours, conditions and bonuses. He knew he needed them to carry the business and they knew he needed them. To oppose their requests and demands would, he believed, make him appear uncooperative, and this he feared would be held against him. He was fearful of their power but would do nothing to oppose it. They took what he willingly gave them but became complacent which resulted in the loss of business. Similarly, the owner of a printing company for whom I conducted a series of telemarketing seminars, prided himself in the fact that his company was a family affair and all who worked in it were part of the happy family. The truth was far away from his perception. His management style was autocratic, he criticised people on a personal level, expected people to work overtime with no reward or praise, and failed to listen to the grievances of his staff or customers. People were motivated by fear, did the minimum required and lost interest in their work and customers. His 'Daddy knows best' approach caused his company to be the first to fail in what was already a shrinking marketplace. The desire to appear cooperative and powerful in these cases were typical examples of how feelings and attitudes – despite hardworking personnel and sophisticated technology – were sufficiently powerful to damage business.

Apathy, laziness and unconcern

The sales manager of a pneumatics company was nearing retirement. His organisation had identified that telemarketing could improve and enhance much of the field sales activity which was taking place, and had announced plans to introduce a call centre. The sales manager was against automation because he felt he was too old to learn new technology. He knew he had a reasonable pension to look forward to and was no longer really motivated in his work. The company were doing well as their product was superior to much of the competition and decided to 'carry' the sales manager by leaving him in position rather than facing the direct and indirect costs of letting him go early. Whether the company decision or the manager's own views were to blame, the fact was that this manager felt lazy, apathetic and unconcerned.

COMMUNICATION

The term 'communication' can mean so many different things. The best global definition could be 'the transfer of information where understanding occurs'. The key word being, understanding.

Communication in the context of customer service deals with the successful transfer of boardroom missions through to front line staff's understanding and behaviour. But a chain is only as strong as its weakest link. One of the major banks recently introduced a service audit for its customers. Designed to provide added value, it dealt with everything from left-handed cheque books through to readjustment of standing order dates. A comprehensive (and expensive) advertising campaign supported the initiative and thus created the image of genuine interest in the unique needs of individual customers. However, high expectations were replaced with early disappointment when several people called their branches to avail of this service. The promised amendments were delayed or incorrect, staff seemed unaware of what the service should include and attitudes displayed over the telephone suggested that to the staff member, the additional work was an inconvenience. What was responsible for this common problem?

- Lack of, or poor, internal communications?
- Inadequate resources?
- Inappropriate lead time?
- Demotivated or disinterested staff?
- Unrealistic additional work volume?
- Lack of, or poor, management guidance/monitoring?
- Lack of training?
- Fear?

This scenario is repeated across many businesses. The dynamic vehicle advertisements 'supported' by lethargic salespeople, the hotline freephone manned by ill-trained personnel, the campaign response number over-loaded with calls such that long waiting periods of engaged tones are the only welcome.

INTERNAL AUDITING

Auditing a company's customer service performance forms a large part of my work, and regularly proves that money invested in image building or time spent on forming customer service policy is often wasted due to the experience the customer encounters at 'key moments'. This is caused most often by the issues listed above.

The most concerning evidence to regularly emerge is that the people who should identify and know about the problems internally, often do not. Simple questions from an objective outsider unveil much which could easily be discovered internally, but most often isn't due to poor communication, fear and assumption. Until the internal 'house' is in order, it is impossible to expect the external customer to be satisfied. Listed below are some of the basic questions I use during an audit interview:

- Are you motivated in your role?
- Is the department management style autocratic or democratic?
- How much of a sense of achievement do you experience in your day-to-day work?
- Are you regularly praised for a job well done?
- Do you experience a sense of responsibility in your work?
- Is your work varied and interesting?
- Do you see a progressive career path and an opportunity to grow with the company?
- Are you adequately trained to perform your day-to-day job function?
- Are you content with more or less than 50 per cent of department policies?
- In the main, are your working conditions and environment acceptable?
- Do you get full, required support from your individual manager?
- Are there any major personality clashes between you and anyone else in the department?
- Do you and your department work as a team?
- Do other departments work as a team?
- Does your department work as a team with other departments?
- Do senior management work as a team?
- Do you work with clear knowledge of how your job function fits into what others in the department do and with the company's mission and plan?
- Do you understand the department objectives?
- Do you feel under stress more than 40 per cent of your working day?
- Do you more often than not achieve that which you had planned to do at the start of a working day?
- Do you know the opinion held of the company by the majority of external customers?
- Do you believe the company operates with a view that everyone else within the company is a customer to someone else within the company?
- Is your nature passive, assertive or aggressive?
- Are you informed of decisions made by management?
- Do you often work later than you are paid to work?
- Are you happy at work?
- Would you make many changes to the department if you had the authority to do so?
- Do you think the company is customer-focused?

- Do you think there are sufficient resources available for you to do your job effectively?
- Do you know what marketplaces you currently serve?
- Do you know what your customers need and want?
- Do your customers get what they need and want?
- What is the biggest difficulty you experience in your job?
- How often do you have department meetings and how useful are they?
- What could be done to ensure the external customer could be better served?

EMPOWERMENT

Empowerment of people within organisations involves balancing managerial control with an employee's freedom to act, so as to bring about greater productivity and improved customer satisfaction. It is a managerial responsibility to commence the steps towards empowerment. Structures, relationships and attitudes are the three key areas which need examination in those steps.

In an empowered organisation:

- One looks not to the boss for direction, but to everyone, including yourself;
- You feel you really do make a difference;
- You feel part of a team;
- You are able to use your full talents and abilities;
- You have control over how you do your job;
- You take initiative;
- You are excited about your work – not negative, suspicious or unwilling;
- The customer is at the centre of what is done;
- Everyone is cooperative;
- Responsibility, skills, authority and control are shared;
- Change can and does happen quickly;
- Power comes from the ability to influence and inspire, not from position or title;
- Tasks and procedures are clearly organised;
- People are trusted and respected;
- People are treated fairly, rewarded for effort and care for each other;
- People are kept informed, problems shared and involvement in decisions encouraged.

Empowerment involves change within:

- Individual attitudes;
- Team behaviour; and
- Organisational values

One without the others will ensure failure. As I often say to clients who are either uninformed or seeking a scapegoat, 'sending your people on a customer service course with me will help, but will not singularly bring about the change you require. For empowerment to take place, changes from within the organisation and management also need to happen.' This is a bitter pill to swallow, and as with many things worth having it involves hard work. Easy come, easy go! Motivation plays a major part in empowerment and is examined in detail in Chapter 7.

A SIMPLE SOLUTION

The solution to many communication problems can be identified very simply. Much of what 'goes wrong' is centred around how people feel. What we say comes from what we think, but what we do comes from how we feel. Consider some examples of the effects of an individual manager's feelings upon his or her staff as shown in Table 5.1.

Managers are 'only human' and will find it doubly difficult to admit their feelings to their staff. Sometimes it isn't even possible to admit these feelings to themselves. But it is a fact that damage can be done in a relationship in a single instant or encounter and be remembered for a

Table 5.1 A manager's feelings, and staff response

The Manager		*The Staff Member*	
Feeling	*Behaviour*	*Feeling Result*	*Behaviour Result*
Superior	Talks down to subordinates	Belittled	Irresponsibility
Threatened	Failure to admit faults or errors	Contempt	Disinterest
Angry	Unfair overspill	Humiliation	Demotivated
Out of depth	Lack of direction	Unimportant	Lack of care
Out of touch	Self-protection	Unrecognised	No achievement desire

long time. Managerial qualities such as integrity, honesty, stability, self-understanding and humility can prevent the negative emotions from being present in the first instance, and thus in the subsequent behaviours. Simple, maybe, but not easy.

Nevertheless, the manifest result of the manager's and employee's behaviour ultimately affects the treatment received by the customer.

Organisations seek the cure through customer service, employee relations and empowerment programmes. I believe the solution sought is in the cause, not the cure.

TEAMWORK

On many occasions I have been asked to conduct a course in teamwork. There are numerous publications available on the subject. Teamwork is synonymous with exemplary customer service, but teamwork is not a tangible 'off the shelf' thing which can be learned or bought. Once again, it is the successful enmeshment of attitudes, behaviour and organisational policy. Teamwork involves a group of individuals working together towards a common goal. The result is improved productivity and harmony. Some describe it as *synergy*, meaning that the sum of the whole is greater than the sum of the individual parts. And, once again, teamwork is centred around how people feel.

Below is a checklist of factors which are in place if a group of people are actually working together as a team. It maybe a useful benchmark for your organisation or department:

- Its members share explicit common objectives;
- It produces in output terms more than the sum of its individual parts;
- Members participate willingly in tackling individuals' problems;
- It isn't leader-dependent, in the sense that all members share responsibility for success and failure;
- A flexible and explicit working procedure exists which all members adhere to;
- It allocates time to process issues, for example, leadership, structure, relationships, objectives or working procedures;
- Openness between members is such that relationship issues can be discussed in a mature way at any time;

- Over a period of time individual contribution levels are more or less equal;
- Its members learn while they work;
- It thinks 'results' first then 'method', but acknowledges that both are equally important;
- Each member values and respects the contribution of the others;
- Each member can and does use the other members (including the leader) as a resource;
- Disagreements are worked through by discussion;
- The use of voting procedures is sparing and normally only as a last resort;
- Members enjoy team meetings.

What causes much frustration and is evidenced by the cries of many people I meet during my work, is that most often individuals desperately want to be part of a team but are not empowered by opportunity, authority or position to create the necessary factors or changes necessary for teamwork to take place and grow.

For example, in one large organisation with whom I worked, all the complaints letters are dealt with by just one individual working in the multi-staffed customer service department. To acknowledge the letters promptly is easy for this person. To later reply with a comprehensive and factual grasp of the situation is more difficult for him because it inevitably involves discussion and communication with other personnel who would have been involved in transactions leading up to the complaint. Other people do not have time to work with him or respond to his investigation requirements because they are 'too busy' completing work upon which their success is separately judged – either by the customer or management. His task of responding within the decreed senior management deadline is frustrated by delays imposed by colleagues' different priorities. This person wants to work as a team with his contemporaries to deal with complaints effectively and efficiently, but the climate is not right for him to do so.

In another company, the telesales staff believed attrition could be prevented if a simple progress call could be made to clients after service supply. Problems only came to light if the client telephoned, but in many instances the customer merely called a new or different supplier. The telesales team wished desperately for this follow-up policy – even to the point where they were prepared to do it themselves. But management wanted them to concentrate upon selling. Their proposal for another department to take on the task of follow-up calls was denied by management. Their desire to work as a team with others to provide complete and meaningful customer service was once again frustrated by their environment. I often meet this scenario where those closest to the customer see a solution but others somewhat removed and with different 'agendas' seem completely disinterested. The common cry is 'we do not have sufficient resources'; however, working more effectively with existing resources is often the solution to the problem.

A third example of the unfulfilled desire to work better as a team came from the personnel and training manager of a large pharmaceutical company. She carried the responsibility of designing training programmes for all departments, including customer services. The programme undoubtedly filled obvious gaps and would have resolved many of the issues about which customers were complaining. The customer service manager was unprepared to release the staff for training as it would mean 'less personnel covering telephones which are overloaded at full complement'. The training did not proceed and the personnel and training manager who had been prepared to work as part of the customer service team was left barren in her ability to solve the problem. Although the customer service department was a customer of the training department, the supplier in this case was unable to complete the customer's requirement.

LOYALTY THROUGH CUSTOMER SERVICE

Losing a customer may not mean just one purchase. Measured as a lifetime revenue the loss can be far more costly. An individual who spends £50 in the same supermarket every week for just ten years would amount to a loss of £20 800!

Exceeding the customer's expectations is undoubtedly an excellent definition of customer service; however, whether this automatically leads to repeat business and loyalty is questionable. Just because customers are now greeted with a smile doesn't guarantee they won't defect to the competition if, for example, there are delays in delivery. *Discovering* that a more prompt delivery is of equal importance to the customer – then providing it – is the key to loyalty. Implementing what is thought important by the supplying organisation instead of seeking to discover what the external customer really wants is still a common folly. Simply asking your customer what creates their loyalty and what you can do to increase and extend it is a good place to start!

Loyalty can be recognised by four types of behaviour:

- Making repeat purchases;
- Purchasing across different product and service lines;
- Giving referrals;
- Demonstrating an immunity to the attraction of the competition.

To achieve this goal, the supplier needs to develop a mix of marketing, research, employee training and motivation techniques. Research to reveal the level of repeat purchases, volume of purchases, number of referrals, degree of competitive activity and what are the aspects of the product or service itself which encourage loyalty. Learning the kinds of pull from competitors which are likely to succeed through surveys, focus groups, mystery shopping and cross-industry analysis. Sales and service training, effective database management and marketing communications programmes all combine to produce the necessary information (which must then be shared at **all** levels of the supplying organisation) to encourage loyalty. The so called customer satisfaction index becomes the new customer-loyalty index.

UNDERSTANDING CHANGE

To achieve lasting and realistic change in customer service policies and internal communications involves knowing about change itself and how change affects people. Resistance to change and the psychology behind it is a good starting point. Most humans resist change because of a feeling of threat to security. The extent to which we feel secure is mainly dependent on our cumulative experiences since birth and, whilst deeply ingrained, we are not often entirely conscious of them. Seven primary factors determine how an individual feels about change:

1. Post birth experiences, for example feeding, weaning, toilet training, sibling rivalry etc.
2. Current personal circumstances, for example marital, health and financial status.
3. Cultural beliefs relating to a country, community, trade, class or work group.
4. Extent of trust and loyalty resulting from past and present (work) relationships with, for example management, union and work groups.

5. Experience of the after-effects of past changes.
6. Specific apprehensions and expectations about the particular change, for example relating to content and method of change for the individual, workgroup and entire organisation.
7. The way in which change is introduced.

Resistance will be less if:

- managers and supervisors are seen to *own* the change and support it wholeheartedly by their own behaviours;
- participants see the change as reducing rather than increasing their current burdens;
- the programme offers the kind of new experience which interests the participants;
- participants feel their autonomy is not threatened;
- change is in accord with values and ideals long-acknowledged by the participants;
- participants have been involved in all levels of diagnostic efforts leading them to agree upon the problem and its importance;
- the project is adopted by consensus following group discussion;
- parties involved can see both sides of a question and recognise valid objections;
- provision is made for the ongoing feedback of views and ongoing clarification recognising that change can become misinterpreted;
- participants begin to experience trust and confidence in one another;
- change is treated as a group process involving participation;
- it involves collaborative relationships;
- it uses consensus; and
- it requires involvement and participation of members in monitoring and evaluating the effects of change.

The managing director of a chocolate factory still personally signs and sends birthday cards to all his employees. The chief executive of a multi-national computer company has installed a telephone line directly to his desk for use only by employees with suggestions for improvement within the company, and Richard Branson of Virgin telephones customers personally when they have had cause to complain. These are all examples of change but, most importantly, change from the top. Only when employees see senior personnel genuinely involved will they make their own serious commitment to change.

QUALITY ISSUES

'Quality is making money out of satisfying customers. Quality comes first.'   (Sir John Egan)

'Quality is everyone's job . . . Quality is essential just to stay in the race.'   (John F: Akers)

'Quality is putting the customer first every time.'
(Colin Marshall)

Quality is still an all-important issue in customer service. Many organisations embark upon Total Quality Management programmes but these can fail for two simple reasons:

1. It becomes a gimmick – 'flavour of the month'.
2. It becomes a fantasy – no tangible means of implementation.

Total quality is all about *getting it right the first time*. The traditional approach to quality could be described as 'test and fix' in that it allows mistakes to be made and builds in expensive procedures for correction, for example quality control departments. IBM Japan's reaction to a customer specifying allowable defects within an order was:

'We Japanese have a hard time understanding North American business practices, but the 3 defective parts per 10 000 have been included and are wrapped separately.'

Traditional quality has no agreed definition. The total quality approach, however, does. It agrees the requirements of customers now and in the future and is precise and measurable, that is it overcomes the vagueness of the past.

Total quality recognises that the customer is no longer just the end-user, there is also the internal customer, that is each department within a company is a customer of another one. Perfection isn't really expensive. If one considers the economics of total quality versus traditional quality, 'the fewer the faults, the higher the cost' whereas with total quality 'the fewer the faults, the lower the cost'.

The average amount of management time spent upon the mismanagement of quality is approximately 35 per cent. 80 per cent of the problems come from 20 per cent of the causes.

The five reasons why so many companies have problems with quality are:

1. They don't do things correctly.
2. There are no follow-up support mechanisms for when things go wrong.
3. There are no clear performance standards.
4. Management do not understand the cost of quality mismanagement.
5. Management do not accept responsibility, and allocate blame to everyone but themselves.

Here are some benchmarks when planning to implement total quality into an organisation:

- Staff need to relate and identify with the customer in large organisations, decentralisation aids the introduction of TQM.
- The success and progress of TQM depends on management.
- Upwards, downwards and sideways communications must be clear, open and politically free.
- Everyone in an organisation must 'own' the process, and this comes mainly from the knowledge that their ideas are recognised.

A statement of 'what we're here to do' is vital. In order to get everyone working towards the same aim, people must:

- understand,
- believe in, and
- use

the statement. If the sense of mission diminishes, so does the pride of the workforce and profits. Corporate culture is about the way we're going to do it, that is organised mechanisms to help people become involved.

The four absolutes of TQM are:

1. *Definition*: what are we here to do and how are we going to do it?
2. *Systems*: all should be geared to improvement
3. *Performance standards*: defined, set levels of operation.
4. *Measurement*: monitoring and reporting, which ensures control is possible. Also measurement of customer satisfaction and loyalty.

Authority should be delegated to the lowest level possible. Responsibility is one of the most powerful motivators – if people own the process and the problem, then inspection is not necessary.

Some methods of working towards TQM are:

- quality education,
- quality department/groups,
- quality circles (mindmaps, fishbone diagrams),
- Customer-care training,
- Business process management,
- Process analysis,
- Departmental activity analysis,
- Customer service teams,
- Quality improvement teams, and
- Personal development training.

And through workshops such as the following:

1. The need for quality improvement;
2. The concepts of quality improvement;
3. The identification of requirements;
4. The measurements of conformance;
5. The prevention of non-conformance;
6. The need for a performance standard;
7. The price of non-conformance;
8. The elimination of non-conformance;
9. The team approach to problem elimination;
10. The company's role in causing improvement;
11. The manager's role in causing improvement;
12. The supplier's role in causing improvement.

The benefits of TQM are:

- extra profits;
- more secure jobs;
- satisfied employees;
- overall more successful;
- reduced haste;
- not the same problems every day;
- increased motivation/morale;
- increased competitiveness;
- enhanced company image;
- increased market share;
- increased productivity;
- reduced time-wasting.

Tom Peters, famous presenter and author of books such as 'in Search of Excellence', suggests the eight secrets of successful quality and service are:

1. Action orientation.
   The 'do it, fix it, try it' approach as opposed to 'analyse it, complicate it, debate it to death' syndrome.
2. Always stay close to your customers.
3. Encourage practical autonomy within your company.
4. Gain productivity through putting your people first.
5. Adopt a 'hands on, value driven' approach; that is, pay attention to values.
6. Do away with hierarchy.
7. Stick to what you know.
8. Ensure rigidity but allow room to innovate.

6 Recruiting and Targeting Telebusiness Personnel

PERSON SPECIFICATION

On more occasions than I care to remember a client would complain when a role was being badly performed that the culprit was 'never right in the first place'. On many of these occasions training was the successful answer; however, if the process of recruitment had been accurately performed in the first instance, problems later on could be avoided.

There are usually four main reasons why the recruitment process fails:

1. The workload from the vacant position is causing an overload for other members of staff to cover. To prevent the low morale which can result from this problem long-term 'the best available at the time' is offered the position, even if they are not the ideal candidate.
2. If an individual is not engaged within a given time frame, the budget allocation for the attached salary is deleted. The remainder of the staff are then expected to absorb the workload.
3. The interviewers are often managers who do not perform the activity on a regular basis, thus the lack of expertise results in a weak interview and often an inappropriate candidate being offered the position. Similarly, in larger organisations the interview may be conducted by members of the personnel department who, although competent at regular interviewing, may not have a sufficiently in-depth knowledge of how the role needs to be performed for it to be completed successfully.
4. Whilst the gap may not be too wide between the skills of the successful applicant and those required to perform the role effectively, lack of or poor training leads to the applicant failing to achieve the full role requirements. This in turn leads to poor productivity, impoverished customer service, training too late, lack of motivation and the 'blame' syndrome.

So the basic rules are:

1. Don't offer the job in haste. Far better to bear the short-term inconvenience of waiting for the right applicant than living with the long-term consequences of the wrong one.
2. Ensure that performance standards, objective appraisal mechanisms, work-flow processes, service benchmarks and best practice policies are in place. A case to the board as to the cost *saving* of holding the position for the right applicant, based upon the facts above, is unlikely to be rejected.
3. Ensure a capable and informed person conducts the interview. Use a team of interviewers if necessary and bear the small cost of buying in outside expertise if necessary, rather than the bigger cost of a square peg recruited for a round hole.
4. Ensure adequate and appropriate induction and ongoing training is provided.

LACK OF MATURITY?

Having met thousands of people performing various telebusiness roles, one of the biggest factors to emerge regarding performance failure has been commercial or biological immaturity. It is not 'wrong' for the individual to be either of these – once again a question is raised regarding recruitment criteria and processes – but it is wrong for the organisation or manager to fail to provide the tools needed to develop the necessary maturity.

Commercial awareness in the context of telebusiness means:

- Displaying awareness of the needs of the customer;
- Projecting an image commensurate with that which the organisation promotes;
- Using language and vocabulary tailored to each individual conversation;
- Ensuring that information gathering is done in such a way that the customer feels an interest in him, not just as a provider of information for a database;
- Understanding the product or service and meaning of branding;
- Taking the initiative; being proactive and confident without being over assertive;
- Showing interest in, and listening to, the caller;

- Conveying an underlying appreciation of how supply aids resolution of a customer's problem – not just increasing order values.

I recently telephoned an Association with the following fairly clear objectives:

1. To determine whether I could obtain some specific information.
2. To identify more fully the aims and objectives of the Association.
3. To then identify the costs and receipts of membership – with a view to joining.

The call proceeded:

> '*I'd like some general information about your Association please. Can you help or put me through to someone who can?*'
> 'Is it a membership inquiry?'
> '*Amongst other things, yes . . .*'
> 'Well I can send you an information pack. What's your name and address?'
> *Provided*
> 'Where did you hear of us?'
> '*I can't recall originally, I've known of your existence for some time. Actually I would like to know a little more about the Association*'
> 'It will all be in the pack. What business are you in?'

At this point I was a little aggrieved that the telephonist clearly wanted to gain information from me for her database and get rid of the call as soon as possible. Had I gained the information I required, I may have been in a position to decide upon membership during the call. I was irritated by the abruptness plus the obvious attempt to obtain the information for the database fields. I proceeded:

> '*This is actually just a general enquiry . . .*'
> (Interrupting) 'Well shall I just put down consultant?'

I gave up then and concluded the call! The way it was handled broke all the rules of displaying appropriate commercial awareness.

ANALYSING THE JOB AND THE PERSON

More and more organisations require telemarketing personnel to deal with a telephone call and input or access data on a computer screen concurrently. The requirement for a new skill is thus emerging. The ability to assimilate audio and visual information is not automatic and can be difficult to assess in an interview situation. At the time of writing this book I know of only one organisation with the facility to test this ability accurately.

Sources of standard recruitment processes include employee recommendations, professional and executive registers, private employment agencies, internal transfers and promotions, universities, technical colleges, selection consultants, the Internet, the personnel department and, of course, advertising. Prior to any interview it is essential to plan, and this starts by evaluating the requirements of the role and the individual. The aim of a job analysis is to provide a clear idea of the requirements of the position to be filled. The end-product is the job description which looks like this:

Job Title	Official name of position
Date	
Location	Geographical position of office, etc.
Purpose	The reason why the post exists
Responsible to	Name of person to whom job holder reports
Responsible for	Name of person or people who report to job holder
Other relationships	Outside the vertical line structure or organisation
Duties & responsibilities	The list of tasks which make up the job. To include regular and occasional, defined and discretionary, administrative, technical along with required levels of performance and methods of assesment
Limitations	Including financial ceilings, budgets, decision-making etc.
Working conditions	To include, for example, out-of-office visits to clients
Pay & terms of employment	To include salary, bonus, hours, holiday entitlement etc.
Training & prospects	To include training plans and career progression

The list of attributes which are essential and desirable in the successful applicant can be drawn up and used to evaluate each candidate:

Physical attributes	Appearance, bearing, voice?
Attainments	Type of education, occupational training?
General intelligence	How much is displayed?
Special aptitudes	Any marked technical ability, manual dexterity, talent?
Interests	Intellectual, practical, physical, social, artistic?
Disposition	Influence over others, self-reliant, dependable?
Circumstances	Domestic situation, other family members, health?

INTERVIEWING

Preplanning of questions before an interview is vital. The following list may assist you to prepare:

- Why did you leave your last job – why do you want to leave your present job?
- What are you looking for in a job?
- Why are you interested in a career/job in . . .?
- What do you think it takes to be a good . . .?
- Do you think you have those characteristics?
- Do you have any specific objectives about things you would like to have or achieve over the next year, three years, ten years. What are they?
- Why should we hire you?
- What are the most outstanding qualities you feel you have that would lend themselves to a successful career in telesales?
- Which of your previous jobs did you enjoy best – what did you like about them?
- Which of your previous jobs did you enjoy the least – what did you dislike about them?
- What do you think has been lacking in your previous jobs that has prevented you from achieving the things you would like to do?

- How do you like to spend your spare time?
- If you were to find the right opportunity, and it required you do some travelling from time to time, how would your family react?
- Would you say that you are generally a lucky person?
- Which of your previous employers could we ring right now for a reference?
- What do you really think that this job entails?
- How can I justify spending so much money on your training?
- Do you really want to commit yourself and pay the price to develop a career? What do you think that really entails?
- What can you do for us that someone else cannot do?
- Describe a difficult problem that you've had to deal with. What have you learned from the jobs you have held?
- What would your references say?
- What type of decisions did you make on your last job? Why were you dismissed?
- In your last job, what were some of the things you spent most of your time on, and why?
- What are the reasons for your success in this profession?
- What is your energy level like? Describe a typical day.
- Why do you want to work here?
- What kind of experience do you have for this job?
- What did you like/dislike about your last job?
- How do you feel about your progress to date?
- How long would you stay with the company?
- What would you like to be doing five years from now?
- What are your qualifications?
- What are your biggest accomplishments?
- Can you work under pressure?
- How interested are you in sport?
- What personal characteristics are necessary for success in your field?
- Do you prefer working with others or alone?
- What difficulty do you have tolerating people with different backgrounds and interests from yours?
- Do you like routine tasks and regular hours?
- Can you take instructions without feeling upset or hurt?
- What kind of things do you worry about?
- What are some of the things you find difficult to do and why do you feel this way?
- What kind of people do you like to work with?

- What kind of people do you find it difficult to work with? How did you get your last job?
- What do you think of your current/last boss?
- Describe a situation where your work or an idea was criticised. What have you done that shows initiative?
- What are some of the things about which you and your supervisor disagreed?
- In what areas do you think your supervisor could have done a better job?
- How well do you feel your boss rated your job performance?
- In what ways has your job prepared you to take on greater responsibility?
- I'm not sure you're suitable for the job.
- What is your greatest weakness?
- What kind of decisions are most difficult for you? Why were you out of work for so long?
- Why aren't you earning more at your age? Why have you changed jobs so frequently? What interests you least about this job?
- What was there about your last company that you didn't particularly like or agree with?
- What is your general impression of your last company? What is your greatest strength?
- What interests you most about this job?
- How much money do you want?
- What are you looking for in your next job?

The poor interviewer can make many mistakes. Try and avoid the following:

Not Preparing

- has made no preparation;
- does not have or know job specification;
- has lost or failed to read candidate's application form;
- gets his/her name wrong;
- no plan, so hops from subject to subject;
- runs out of questions and flounders;
- asks same questions two or three times;
- is constantly interrupted by phone calls etc.;
- makes no notes, writes no assessment, and two days later can recall nothing about the encounter.

Intimidating

- writes notes for two minutes without looking up after candidate enters room;
- barks out questions;
- jumps on apparent discrepancies or inconsistencies;
- tries to show up or catch out candidate;
- gives biscuit and asks crucial question when mouth is full;
- uses military interrogation techniques, walks round candidate shooting questions from the back;
- writes long notes in middle of interview with air of deep significance and hostile judgment.

Agreement Seeking

- looks to candidate to confirm own prejudices or judgment;
- leads him/her to the answer he/she wants;
- finishes off candidates sentences for him/her;
- answers his/her own questions;
- often goes slavishly through application form getting candidate's agreement to all entries.

Wandering

- drifts off point into irrelevancies and red herrings;
- embarks on boring anecdotes which have nothing to do with job in question;
- allows candidate to wander off into irrelevancies too.

Pontificating

- uses interview as excuse for uninterrupted boasting about self or company (or both);
- asks show-off technical questions to which he/she does not know the answer;
- patronises candidate;
- makes up mind on one candidate – ignores all others.

Ducking

- is too polite;
- fails to probe areas which might be unwelcome or embarrassing;
- believes everything candidate tells him/her without probing or checking;
- never probes suspicious claims, facts or gaps in employment dates;
- recommends every candidate for short-list to superior to make decision.

Not Listening

- interviewer sits gazing out of window while candidate talking;
- becomes absorbed in cleaning glasses;
- has few standard questions he/she hasn't changed for years irrespective of candidate or job;
- pays no attention to answers;
- does not realise candidate has stopped talking;
- believes he/she can pick the right person for the job the minute the candidate enters the room;
- does not believe in interviews.
- The interviewer should make it clear when the interview is over and explain what the next step is; that is short list, letter within two weeks, second interview etc.;
- If the candidate has impressed you, give some hint of this, for example: 'clearly your application will have to be taken very seriously';
- If it is obvious the candidate has been unsuccessful, give some hint of this, for example: 'I've got a feeling this isn't really the job for you' – (better than '. . . you're not the person for this job');
- If the candidate is wrong for this job, but a good person for another vacancy, they should be asked if they would be interested in a different job if one came up;
- A note should be taken of the candidate's expenses before they leave;
- The candidate should feel he/she has had a civilised, stimulating conversation which gave every opportunity for them to put their case;
- The interviewer should have available copies of the job specification/ description, and be able to lucidly and briefly summarise the key tasks and responsibilities.

EASY STEPS TO GOOD INTERVIEWING

Step 1: Consider the job.
Step 2: Consider the experience and formal qualifications required.
Step 3: Consider the personal qualities required to carry out the job.
Step 4: Reduce the basic qualifications to no more than four or five.
Step 5: Discuss with other selectors.
Step 6: Consider the application in the light of the formal qualifications and age required.
Step 7: Consider the application in the light of the qualities required.
Step 8: Consider the application to find a 'common link' with the candidate.
Step 9: Examine the application to make sure there are no unexplained gaps in dates.
Step 10: Arrange to reduce or eliminate interruptions.
Step 11: Arrange the seating so that neither interviewer nor candidate is at a disadvantage.
Step 12: Examine your prejudices.
Step 13: Make it immediately clear to the candidate where he/she is to sit etc.
Step 14: Adopt either the 'common link' approach, the 'off balance' approach or a mixture of both.
Step 15: Stop talking yourself.
Step 16: Lead into the groups of subjects you want to discuss.
Step 17: Avoid asking any questions to which he/she can answer 'yes' or 'no'.
Step 18: Question with a purpose.
Step 19: Get at the truth by indirect questioning.
Step 20: Follow up his/her opinions thoroughly.
Step 21: Avoid any tendency to trick the candidate.
Step 22: Tell the candidate something about the job, the terms and conditions.
Step 23: Tell the candidate when they may expect to have the answer to their application.
Step 24: Consider the evidence from the past only as pointers towards the possession of, or lack of, the key qualities you are seeking.
Step 21: Add your own impressions step-by-step.
Step 26: Make up your mind.

PSYCHOLOGICAL TESTING

Psychological or psychometric tests are widely used to support the interview and selection process. Used correctly, as an addition to the interview process, they are most helpful, although inexperienced interviewers should be cautioned not to rely solely upon the findings of these tests.

People can be tested in three ways:

1. *Real life behaviour* – what a person does and has done in a job as judged by his or her performance and the observations of superiors.
2. *Self-ratings* – what the person thinks of their own performance.
3. *Tests* – artificial standardised situations which research has proved give a valid and reliable indication of how a person may be expected to behave in a real life situation.

All tests must be technically sound, administratively convenient and politically defensible before being introduced. A test is only technically sound if it is suited to the individual or group taking it, and if research has shown that it offers a reliable and valid way of assessing abilities, interests or personality traits that distinguish between success and failure, satisfaction and dissatisfaction in the particular job. Tests may only be suited to young people, or for people with a certain level of education, occupational or cultural background, or to certain ability levels. The test must be fair and not too hard or easy.

The test shouldn't take too long to take or mark, and the need for quiet and no interruptions must be taken account of. It should be accepted by managers, applicants and the organisation. Belief in the value of the test is important as is a full and detailed explanation as to why it is being used.

PERFORMANCE STANDARDS

Once the successful candidate is in place it is important to ensure as soon as possible a full understanding not only of the role to be performed but also of the standard at which the employee is expected to operate.

A performance standard is a statement of the conditions which will exist when a duty or responsibility has been (or is being) *satisfactorily* performed. It is:

1. Quantitatively expressed;
2. Devoid of vague, ambiguous language – that is, 'efficient', 'prompt';
3. Attainable because it is feasible and achievable;
4. Committed to by the performer; and
5. Accepted by the performer's supervisor.

Unless all five specifications are met, there is not a performance standard. What can be measured?

- Results
- Symptoms
- Effort

How to measure:

- Quantity
- Quality
- Timeliness
- Cost in managerial performance

What to measure against?

1. Trends – measuring against past performance;
2. Environment – measuring against what others are doing;
3. Requirements – measuring against those things that the company's objectives make mandatory.

Performance standards are a multi-purpose tool for both performers and supervisor, and for their inter-relationships. They are tools for:

1. Releasing the performer's initiative whilst strengthening the supervisor's control.
2. Obtaining the performer's commitment to personal responsibility and the supervisor's acceptance of that commitment.
3. Self-analysis for the performer against performance yardsticks agreed to by the supervisor.
4. Management at all levels to assess performance of others.
5. All levels of the organisation to reach continuous agreement on companywide objectives and methods.
6. Identifying problems,
   (a) when performance deviates from standards, and
   (b) when changes in standards are indicated.

See also Table 6.1.

Table 6.1   Performance standards

Activities '*I do these things*' (*job description*) (*format – 'I + transitive verb + object*')	Purposes '*. . . for these purposes*' (*individual and company objectives*) (*format – 'in order that/ to . . .*')	Standards '*. . . as evidenced by these conditions*' (*performance standards*) (*format – performance is satisfactory when . . .*)
Examples:		
1. I submit proposals for marketing programmes	In order to get them approved promptly and efficiently	When x per cent of them are approved, after not more than y revisions within not more than z days, after initial submission
2. I handle customer complaints	In order to achieve customer satisfaction at the lowest cost in time, money and effort	When not more than x per cent of complaints per year are dealt with by higher authority and not more than y result in additional costs
3. I review cost reports	In order to see that variances are either eliminated, or explained promptly to my supervisor	When my superior does not bring to my attention more than x times a year that he was given accurate, meaningful, or timely information on variances

Note: When there are more than three purposes to an activity, break down that activity. When the same purpose reappears in three or more activities, combine activities. Standards should cover all the purposes listed for each activity.

PERFORMANCE REVIEW

In due course an evaluation of the standard of work being performed is critical both for the organisation and the employee. Everyone likes to know whether they are achieving, under- or over-achieving that which is expected of them. A formal appraisal is the best method.

Contrary to most people's belief, performance appraisal was introduced and designed to be a motivational experience for both the involved parties. Unfortunately, what it has become in many companies is exactly the opposite – a totally de-motivational experience! The reasons for this are many and varied but among the main are:

1. the fact that it has become the *annual* event; and
2. often the appraiser is:

   - ill-prepared,
   - ill-trained in this important activity, and therefore
   - de-motivated before it starts.

3. Often the subordinate is:

   - ill-prepared usually because he/she has not been invited to prepare,
   - de-motivated before the event starts because of previous bad experiences, and
   - unhappy that 'God-like' judgments are going to be passed on his/her previous period's work.

4. Often the appraisal is:

   - held in the wrong environment,
   - in the wrong atmosphere.

The primary purpose of an appraisal is to *help* the subordinate, and reasons for appraisals are:

- to provide knowledge of individual performance;
- to plan for future promotions and successions;
- to assess training and development needs;
- to provide information for salary planning and special awards; and
- to contribute to corporate career planning.

Everything written should be shown and shared

- secrecy breeds suspicion, and
- suspicion destroys a counselling relationship.

Two specific aspects often withheld are those relating to poor performance and potential promotion.

In the first, the secrecy reflects the manager's own anxiety – telling someone they are doing badly is not easy. The second, promotion, is difficult as telling the subordinate of potential promotion is very likely to be interpreted as definite, with keen disappointment if it does not happen.

If there is something a manager feels they cannot communicate to a subordinate, then that is probably a good enough reason to exclude it from the appraisal report.

'The appraisal report should be finalised in the presence of the subordinate.'

'The subordinate should contribute a major part to the appraisal.'

Self-appraisal is particularly effective in two areas. First, the area of weak performance – most individuals will be surprisingly open and honest about themselves if the appraisal/counselling is a supportive relationship. Secondly, the area of career progression – managers tend to see a subordinate's future in terms of the other people in the department and how, particularly, the manager' s own progression developed. Giving the subordinate the chance to talk may reveal totally different aspirations.

Emotion

There is always an element of emotion in appraisal interviewing. Both manager and subordinate each have positive and negative feelings, and appreciating what they are can help understanding.

The Manager

Positive feelings:
- Want to be helpful and understanding but may be inclined to offer advice too closely related to their own experience. Need to remember the subordinate is an individual in their own right.
- Want to be kind and tolerant and liked by their staff. However, they must be prepared to point out the realities of any situation.

Negative feelings:
- May be fearful of the interview itself and whether they may make a mess of it. Will diminish with practice.
- Fear of interview getting emotional and perhaps creating hostility in the subordinate. Overcome by developing relationships where expression of feelings is normal.

- May have feelings of envy (subordinate's youth, health, qualifications or career opportunities). Must control them.

The Subordinate

Positive feelings:
- Want to be liked by the boss. Must not allow this to make themselves dependent and subservient.
- Want to be helped to improve.

Negative feelings:
- The most likely is fear of criticism of work or behaviour. Until this fear is allayed by the manager, the interview will be meaningless and achieve nothing. Only the manager can allay this fear by establishing a counselling relationship which shows he/she is fair and can be trusted.

So how should a performance appraisal be run to ensure that it is a practical and motivational experience?

1. Annual appraisals are too far apart. At best the appraisal should be quarterly – at worst twice annually.
2. Advise staff well in advance:

    - get the subordinate to complete a copy of the appraisal form on him/herself;
    - one question that should be included in every appraisal document is 'How well was I managed this year?'

3. The appraiser should prepare properly by:

    - reviewing the period's results;
    - studying the last appraisal result;
    - checking the appraisee's personal file and job description;
    - talking to any other managers who have been involved;
    - complete outline copy of appraisal.

4. The appraisal interview:

    - As both appraiser and appraisee have completed the form, the interview is not the appraiser telling the appraisee what the company (or appraiser) thinks of him/her, but is a discussion about the points of agreement and a negotiation about the points of variance.
    - The appraiser should get and keep the appraisee talking, and concentrate on listening.

- When the evidence has been brought to light they can then go on to diagnose the areas of problems. It is vital that the diagnosis concentrates on things which can be improved, not on basic character traits.
- When the problem areas have been faced up to, an agreed appraisal can then be written and signed by both parties.
- It is now possible to move on to the most vital stage which is to agree a plan of action to overcome the problems. This plan should be time-targeted.
- If the interview is to be effective it must not be confused with a salary review. That is quite a separate interview.

5. After the interview:

- Appraiser to complete any other paperwork straight away; and
- the action plan should be progressed and monitored on a regular basis.

6. In the event of agreement not being possible the appraisee should have the right to a further interview by the appraiser's superior.

TARGETING

Agreeing the amount of business likely to be gained and generated by a telesalesperson is sound business practice. Any company must have regular planning to control its rate of growth and to relate its revenue and profits to the market return on investment.

A company should never get into a position where it is:

- Selling more products than it can provide.
- Selling less products than production has planned to produce.
- Selling a 'product mix' which is out of line with the best manufacturing mix.
- Selling a mix of products which is out of line with the market.

Thus, the company must set sales objectives. To be effective they should be:

1. *Quantitative* – the objectives should be amounts of money or numbers of units.
2. *Measurable* – so that monitoring of performance can be set against budget and indicate variances.

3. *Specific* – each salesperson must know what his/her objectives are, and to which period they relate.
4. *Attainable* – too high and the salesperson is de-motivated. Too low and they fail to realise their full potential.
5. *Related to* – if the company operates an incentive scheme.

If a sales force is merely given an arbitrary set of targets to meet for the next year, there is a very good chance of trouble within the ranks. Only when each salesperson has estimated the potential business for their area, discussed it with the sales manager and finally agreed on the targets, will he or she accept *accountability* for achieving those targets.

'I reckon I can increase this year's figures by 20 per cent!'
'I think I might manage an additional 5 per cent'
'Surely you don't think we're going to get increased business with the sort of recession I've got in my area?'

Three typical statements – cases of 'think of a number and double it!' There is only one way to prepare a meaningful forecast and that is properly. Detail, detail and more detail, and it is not a job that can be done in a few hours. In fact, two or three months may be nearer the mark. Increased business can only come from two areas:

- more business from existing customers, and
- business from new customers.

We already have (or should have) a breakdown of current and past business from existing customers, and that gives us our baseline from which to work. Deal with each grade of accounts in turn starting with grade A down to grade C (or even D).

1. By using either available computer software or a simple list format, itemise in detail all probable (and attainable) business from existing customers.
2. The best person to give the salesperson an indication of order quantity/value next year is the customer.
3. If the customer will not supply the information then a calculated guess from past history will do. Bear in mind competitors' activities.
4. Finally, new business. With no records available estimates have to be guessed, but the salesperson should, over the past year, have been compiling a Prospect List. Estimates can be based on factors such as

size of prospect, type of business, competitors' activities, and so on. If the salesperson does not already get an analysis of monthly orders for his/her territory then the sales office should be asked to provide it. The sales manager should go through the analysis with the salesperson, pinpointing signs which might indicate growth (or recession) over the next 12 months.

Once all sales people in the team have agreed on their targets it is quite simple for the manager to produce a forecast of totals. It is vital that variances between targets and actuals are discussed with the salesperson as soon as they show up so that corrective action can be taken. These variances may be in the value of orders received, or of an imbalance of product mix – either will affect the year-end figures.

Forecasting is not an exact science, but provided everyone reads historical data correctly and projects forward realistically, the element of luck is considerably reduced.

INCENTIVE SCHEMES

Views on the value of incentivisation do vary. Many people believe money is the only motivator, whereas others are firmly convinced otherwise. Let's look at financial incentives first. Would you agree or disagree with the following statements?

'Performance-geared remuneration is an unnecessary stimulant for good, conscientious sales people. A good -sized salary instead is better.'

This is unlikely. What makes good, conscientious salespeople stay that way is the recognition element of being rewarded for performance. So long as the salary is commensurate with the required standard of performance, good salespeople will be encouraged to do even more than the minimum if they are given an added incentive to do so.

'In many companies, financial incentives cannot be used as there is no sensible basis for establishing commissions.'

This is not true. In every situation it is possible to provide some form of performance-related incentive – so long as the performance standard has been clearly set and understood in the first instance.

'Well-designed and properly planned incentives have no negative side effects.'

This should be true although a caution must be made. Variance plays a large part in motivating. The same thing repeated over and over again can become demotivating. Others not involved in the incentive scheme may raise negativity, and consistently failing to achieve the performance required to attain the incentive may also be demotivational.

'Sizeable annual bonuses may have considerable influence on sales performance.'

A bonus paid 'as a matter of course' does not carry the same feelings value as one earned as a result of specific activity. An annual bonus may be too long in coming – many organisations pay an equivalent bonus quarterly or six-monthly. So long as those who contribute to the achievement of the bonus are those involved in being paid it, an annual bonus is a good incentive. Don't forget, however, the old adage, 'a reward once given becomes a right'. Whilst it might be paid one year as a result of exceeding target, it will be expected next year even if the target is only barely achieved.

There are five main rules to ensure an incentive scheme is effective and genuine:

1. It should contain a variable element strong enough to stimulate efforts or performance beyond the average and provide a corresponding-ingly important difference in income.
2. The scheme should also encompass effective use of time. Does it reward what should and is meant to be rewarded?
3. It should influence the natural motivation of the salesperson, without jeopardising the objectives of the company.
4. It should be fair and equitable.
5. It should be good business for the company.

Telemarketing teams vary. In some instances the individuals enjoy and prefer to work in an environment of competitive rivalry where individual achievement is promoted, published and separately rewarded. In other situations, the ethos is different in that all the team prefer to be measured and judged collectively. In the first instance, therefore, individual incentives are more appropriate, in the second a team incentive works better. Investigating and identifying the type of atmosphere is the key to deciding which works best, and only the skilled manager is able to operate both systems!

7 Managing and Training Telebusiness Personnel

THE ROLE OF THE TELEBUSINESS MANAGER

The role of the sales office manager is to achieve the objectives and tasks of the sales office through the sales office team.

The objectives and tasks of the sales office are to support the long-term management of the organisation, to integrate with other business areas, to assist the success of the field sales team by ensuring the availability of relevant information and to deal with all sales-related issues and processes quickly and effectively.

MOTIVATION

Telebusiness personnel are no different to other personnel in the respect that they are human and therefore respond to the same motivational factors. Much has been researched and written about the subject and I will attempt to combine the best of all theories.

Motivation is not something we do for half an hour on a Tuesday afternoon! It is an ongoing process combining practical activities along with managerial attitudes and behaviours. On courses, when a manager tells me their staff are not motivated, I ask, 'how well are they managed?', because an effective manager invests time to ensure staff are working in an environment in which they can be self-motivated. Self-motivation is not the only kind of motivation; however, it is a manager's responsibility to ensure the factors which cause motivation are present.

The definition of motivation is 'anything which causes action', and the source can of course be positive or negative. Fear is a motivator, and was historically much-used and known as the 'carrot and stick' approach. The problem with this form of motivation is it only produces unwillingness and the bare minimum of productivity. People only do enough to avoid that which they are fearful of – and no more. In today's enlightened world it is recognised that if a climate of willingness can be created, individuals will produce results far above the minimum. In today's competitive society, the minimum is not enough. The goal is to have motivated workforces producing above average results.

Maslow's theory of motivation is quite famous. He maintains that we all operate within a constantly changing hierarchy of needs which are felt with decreasing strength as they ascend. Our most base needs such as food and sleep are physical, followed closely by the need for security – be it emotional, financial or physical. The next tier is the need and desire for recognition either in the form of praise, acceptance or approval from others. The desire to lead follows with its potential to manifest in any area of life – anything from being a golf captain to a departmental manager. Finally, what Maslow describes as self-actualisation is the final level within the hierarchy. Doing something just to prove to oneself it can be done. The problem with this theory is that although it helps us to understand how human motivation can work, it doesn't really offer strong practical value.

Douglas McGregor has developed two theories which further explain human behaviour; these are known as theory X and theory Y. Essentially, theory X builds on the lower order of human needs, while theory Y assumes that, once met, these needs no longer motivate. It builds on the higher order of needs. Human behaviour is based on theory – we do A because we theorise it will produce B. Our attitude and approach to managing people is of paramount importance in how they will respond. Our actions produce their reactions. It may therefore be useful to check our own assumptions against the following sets of assumptions.

Theory X

1. The average human being has an inherent dislike of work and will avoid it if possible.
2. Because of the human characteristic of dislike of work, most people must be coerced, controlled, directed or threatened with punishment to get them to put forth adequate effort towards the achievement of organisational objectives.
3. The average human being prefers to be directed, wishes to avoid responsibility, has relatively little ambition and wants security above all.

Theory Y

1. The expenditure of physical and mental effort in work is as natural as play or rest.
2. External control and the threat of punishment are not the only means for bringing about effort towards organisational objectives. People will exercise self-direction and self-control in the service of objectives to which they are committed.
3. Commitment to objectives is related to the rewards associated with their achievement.
4. The average human being learns, under proper conditions, not only to accept but to seek responsibility.
5. The capacity to exercise a relatively high degree of imagination, ingenuity and creativity in the solution of organisational objectives is widely, not narrowly, distributed in the population.
6. Under the conditions of modern industrial and commercial life, the intellectual potentialities of the average human being are only partially utilised.

The need is not so much to choose sides as to which theory is 'right', but to make our assumptions about human behaviour more explicit and to check how well our own behaviour reflects our assumptions. As we treat people, so they behave. If we tell someone they are no good often enough, they are likely to start believing it and act accordingly. Similarly with encouragement, praise and recognition, McGregor's theory suggests they will respond with self-belief and positive behaviour. Theory Y is more dynamic than theory X. It is more optimistic about the possibility for human growth and development, more concerned with self-direction and self-responsibility, and more consistent with available social science knowledge.

Theory X or Theory Y would influence how we organise for decision-making and action. If we accept Theory X, then it would make sense to have:

- One-way communication;
- Strategy-planning by the top leaders only. Decision-making at the top level only;
- A handing down of decisions to be implemented by middle management;
- A handing down of instructions to be carried out by the workers.

Theory Y would make it worthwhile to have:

- Two-way communication;
- Involvement in goal-setting, planning and decision-making at each level.

The most practical theory available comes from the work of Professor Frederick Hertzberg. It stems from two statements:

1. 'What makes people happy and motivated at work, is what they do', and
2. 'What makes people unhappy and de-motivated at work, is the situation in which they do it'.

Hertzberg examined the quality of the working experience. Much as we concentrate upon gaining customer loyalty through effective marketing and customer care practices, Hertzberg claims motivated personnel result from the experience they have at work. This should be cultivated and not just left to happen or evolve. This starts by defining people as they are, not as we want them to be. Constantly I hear on courses, 'We are not like that. Treat me the way I am, not the way you believe me to be'. So managers must face the needs of the people – not their own projected needs.

The first set of needs defined by Hertzberg are called *hygiene factors* which deal with a person's relationship with the environment. They consist of how people are treated at work:

1. Do you pay them well?
2. Do they enjoy good working conditions?
3. Are the human relations right? – the nature and quality of their supervision.
4. Is the company's policy and administration as positive as it can be?

One form of hygiene that has long been practiced is to deny people fair treatment at the beginning. For example: 'I am not going to pay you as much as the going rate, but prove you can do the job, and I will make it up to you later'.

The trouble is that you can never make it up. The lack of fair treatment at the beginning will never be forgotten and normally leads to a revenge psychology on the part of the employee. In other words, they will get back at you later because they cannot forget the remembered pain. The principle here is very simple. Treat people fairly, because it is in your own, and their, best interests.

Hygiene factors are issues which cause people to be demotivated. Arranging for them to be prevented or corrected will eliminate demotivation, but will not be enough to motivate people to want to do more.

The other set of needs are known as the *motivators*. Motivators are variable factors which, if present, cause people to want to do more. They consist of:

- Achievement;
- Recognition for achievement;
- Meaningful and interesting work;
- Increased responsibility; and
- Growth and advancement at work.

In other words – the quality of the human experience at work.

A point that Hertzberg insists is vital is that motivators are not more important than hygiene factors. Equal time should be spent eliminating hygiene factors and creating motivators, as one without the other is only half-effective. In Figure 7.1 everything to the left of 0 represents the strength and duration of the demotivational feeling and effect. Everything to the right of the 0 represents the strength and duration of positive, willing motivational feeling and effect.

One of the most important variables in creating motivation is training, because motivation is a function of ability and the opportunity to use that ability. So the more ability we can give people by training them, the more they will want to do. Once again, there has to be a balance. Promotion (opportunity) without training is demotivational. A new telesales supervisor who is good at selling but has not been trained to manage people will flounder. Attendance on a supervisory skills course for someone who's promotion is unconfirmed or far futuristic, will be equally demotivated.

So, what should a job contain? Hertzberg summarises:

1. A range of responsibilities and activities to keep a person interested.
2. Areas of growth, since all jobs should be a learning experience.
3. Direct feedback, since how a person is doing should not be dependent upon someone else telling them – they should be able to see for themselves.
4. The responsibility for checking one's own quality, because that responsibility cannot be delegated to a control system.
5. Direct communication between that person and the people they need to communicate with, not always via supervisors or managers.

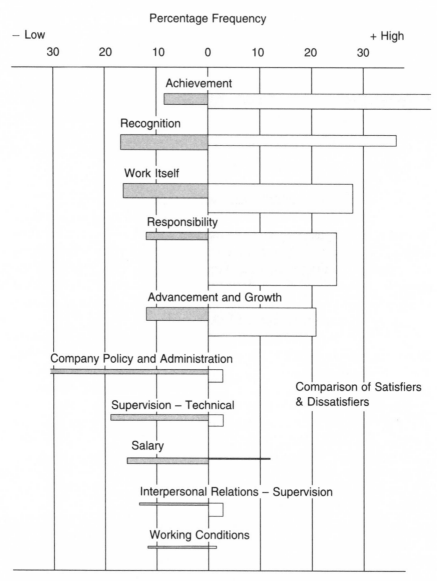

Source: F. Hertzberg, *The Motivation to Work*.

Figure 7.1   The motivation–hygiene theory

To ascertain what can be done to create the correct environment, you may wish to consider your answers to the following questions and compare them with the suggestions listed.

1. How can we give our people more opportunity to achieve?
2. In what different ways can we recognise them when they do achieve?
3. How can we make the job more fulfilling, more satisfying?
4. What can we do to give our people more responsibility?
5. What can we do to help our people advance and grow?

Suggestions are as follows:

- **Achievement**
  Positive and fair targets and objectives.
  Increase individual responsibility.
  Invite involvement of individuals, for example suggestion schemes.
  Increase variety of tasks.
  Individual performance standards.
  Increase freedom to work in own way (whilst retaining control).
  Assess individual abilities.
  Welcome good ideas and introduce where feasible.
  Motivate individuals towards achievements.
  Increase job satisfaction.

- **Recognition**
  Verbal praise when a job is well-done.
  Increase direct communication between workers and management.
  Report excellent achievement to management and get management involved in praise.
  Show their importance by working alongside them from time to time.
  Written recognition for exceptional achievement.
  Hold group discussions/meetings.
  Thank them.
  Ask for their help and opinions.
  Notice the positives.

- **Work itself**
  Improve working conditions, equipment and facilities.
  Diminish frustrations wherever possible.
  Concentrate on developing a team approach.
  Consider job rotation/jobswap.
  Delegate.
  Create a positive environment.
  Ensure own expertise is adequate.

- **Responsibility**
  Increase awareness of individuals' specific responsibilities.
  Encourage self-analysis.
  Measure individual abilities and increase responsibility accordingly.
  Hold group meetings and encourage involvement.
  Give special projects to more experienced staff.
  Widen individual knowledge of total company operation.
  Increase authority.

- **Growth and advancement**
  Training in current job.
  Development training where appropriate.
  Counselling.
  Ensure a career structure and path.
  Increase individual self-confidence
  Promote.

TRAINING AND COACHING

Training is a powerful and underused management tool in many organisations. It is intangible, takes time and is often the 'first thing to go'
when financial or operational pressures loom. Nevertheless, as the old
adage challenges, 'if you think training is expensive, try ignorance'.

The aims when performing the management responsibility of on-job
training are:

1. To assess performance on the job in the light of an existing and
   agreed job description and known standards.
2. To determine strengths and current areas of improvement and secure
   recognition of these.
3. To coach in skills and techniques in which deficiencies have been
   recognised, and impart other knowledge to the extent that this can be
   done effectively on the job.
4. To foster the attitudes of professionalism by example, encouragement
   and instruction.
5. To give specific guidance in the process of self-training which must
   continue in the absence of the manager/trainer.
6. To determine training requirements which may not be fully tackled
   on the job, assessing and reporting on appropriate means of meeting
   them.

7. To evaluate improvements of performance, the effects and methods of training given.
8. To motivate.

Thus the prime function of the trainer/manager is that of **control**.

In the process of fostering a complex skill the manager must:

- Analyse the task in which skills are deficient into units within the intellectual grasp of the person being trained, and ensure that they are understood.
- Set a goal or standard of performance by demonstration (note that the demonstration does not in itself teach a complex skill).
- Initiate trials of the demonstrated skill.
- Indicate success and failure in specific terms.
- Suggest specific improvements.
- Maintain morale during the periods of poor progress which will naturally occur.
- Distribute training time as far as possible in the light of learning patterns revealed by the individual.

It is advisable for the manager to appraise performance observed by means of a carefully designed appraisal form. This will be based upon a detailed breakdown of all those functions and skills listed in the job description which may be observed on the job. The post-appraisal interview, like any other interview, must be given a structure based upon appreciation of the psychology of persuasion. A suitable structure is:

1. *Praise* – show appreciation of all skills well-used.
2. *Ask* – invite analysis of the performance by the person, by questions.
3. *Encourage/tell* – discuss any primary improvement areas which the person has not identified under 2.
4. *Improve* – after agreement of the improvement areas ask the person to suggest methods of improvement.
5. *Help* – if they cannot define improvement methods, help them to find them.
6. *Action* – plan how those improvements can be introduced.
7. *Praise* – finish on a high note by praising again.

It will only be successful if it is in specific terms, it concentrates on technical faults, is largely participative, and avoids general counselling.

The benefits of ongoing coaching and training are for the subordinate:

- A continuous improvement in performance.
- Greater understanding of what they are doing and why.
- Greater confidence in their own ability (a realistic perception because it is highlighted through skill improvement), which in turn can create a willingness to try for more new, and improved quality of, skills.
- A willingness to manage their own weaknesses, and an opportunity to change them into strengths.

For the supervisor/manager all the above areas are relevant if the developmental role is carried up through the organisational structure. But of equal importance, as the subordinate improves his or her performance developing more and more the existing and new-found skills, the performance of the department as a whole will increase. People become more self-motivating, taking greater responsibility for their own development and performance.

In other words, subordinates start to generate their own increase in performance, success breeding success, confidence building more confidence, enabling the supervisor and manager to have more **time** to identity new ways to improve performance, therefore perpetuating an ever-upwards spiral of growth.

How do we help bring this about? To make this process work there is one key element that needs to be added to that of focusing on success. What happens if we feed back error? How do we feel? All we know is what not to do next time, but we are no further forward in knowing what to put in its place! How does this help us? Well it does narrow down our options, but it is a long-winded process and what happens to our confidence and willingness to try new skills and behaviour on the way? From our earliest days at school we are told to concentrate on what we do badly and put it right; how many of us have struggled and struggled with trying to improve skills that we have no talent for, and we don't really understand what's wrong with them anyway!

Of course we need to manage our weaknesses and to build and improve on them, but it's redressing the balance between focusing on weaknesses as opposed to strengths that we need to concentrate on. What happens if we focus on feeding back success? What went well, and why? How do we feel? This time we know that what we did had a positive result, that given similar circumstances we can repeat this action and we will have another success. How does this help us? Well it tells us behaviour/skills that we can repeat, it builds our confidence legitimately because it's based on fact, and it enables us to develop our existing talents/skills which gives us the confidence and time (because we are more effective) to concentrate on developing weaknesses into positive strengths.

Setting Tasks

Every task should have a learning target. This should be agreed between the coach and the trainee prior to any training taking place. It is crucial that the trainee understands why the training/tasks are being undertaken and what benefits are likely to be incurred. They should be made to feel that training is a developmental process, one step on a journey to continually improve their performance.

The coach and trainee should discuss prior to the tasks being set:

● What skills are to be measured.
● How this will take place.
● What constitutes a successful performance.
● How a successful performance will be measured and why.

Each task should therefore be capable of being monitored, for example, with dates, reports, set standards and purposes and so forth.

Each task is set within the trainee's level of ability, experience and developmental needs whilst still remaining challenging. There is nothing more demoralising than continually being set tasks that you cannot complete.

The opportunities for coaching in a telebusiness unit or call centre are both formal and informal. Informal coaching opportunities can be broken down into three areas:

1. Where the operators are persistently seeking information and advice, either on product knowledge or on how to handle an awkward or difficult call. The opportunity exists here for the manager/coach to place the learning firmly back to the subordinate by resisting the temptation to give a ready answer; instead, by asking questions, to encourage the operator to seek their own answers. If time does not allow this to happen, then the coach could follow up later by asking, 'given similar circumstances, what would you do next time?' 'Where could you get that information for yourself?' and so on. These are golden opportunities to improve the performance of your staff which should not be missed.

2. Where the manager/coach spends time walking the job, listening side by side to individuals, and questioning/making suggestions for an improvement in performance, continuously encouraging and supporting the staff and building a 'reservoir of good will'. This can have a dramatic effect upon both the morale of the unit and teamwork as a whole.

3. Where the manager/coach listens in to individual calls without the knowledge of the individual concerned. This can be effective, but consider the other effect it has upon individuals in terms of morale and team building. This management/coaching style instead of developing and nurturing can come across as negative policing if not handled properly.

With regard to formal coaching opportunities, there are two main opportunities:

1. Where the manager/coach works 'side by side' with the clerks at their desks and listening in to their calls, is able to provide them with immediate and specific feedback relating to their performance in a real 'live' situation, thereby improving their quality of performance.

    There are several factors that we need to consider if this purpose is to be achieved. To create the right atmosphere we need to reassure and show that we are there to help, not criticise. Our role is that of a coach, to help develop and improve further their new and existing skills. Therefore we need to fully explain this purpose and continually reinforce the philosophy. Any notes, comments or reports that we are going to make should be shown and discussed, preferably as we go along, if not as soon as possible after training.

    The coaching session itself should last approximately one hour and be broken down:

    - as an introduction/reinforcement of the coach's role and the objectives of the session;
    - to recap on any previous notes, reports or training plans that have been made and to review the trainee's progress to date in those areas;
    - to discuss with the trainee any specific personal needs or requirements he or she may have and where necessary to plan how they can be overcome;
    - to clarify/confirm with the trainee how performance will be measured and in which areas;

- to listen to the trainee for approximately 10 to 15 minutes without interrupting, to allow time for settling down and for data to be collected on their performances;
- to stop the trainee and to discuss any notes regarding their performance. Remember, stick to the facts, be positive and focus on success. Discuss and agree ways that can further improve their performance, make notes (that they can see!) to reinforce the learning, and then listen to some more calls. Review progress, plan to improve and prepare for the next call and so on . . .;
- at the end of the session, summarise the trainee's overall performance. Agree and write down the specific areas the trainee should concentrate upon during the period leading to the next session. Make sure the trainee has a copy of these agreed plans, with targets and standards as appropriate;
- complete the coaching review form and ensure that the supervisor/ manager and the trainee read, sign and make comments as required.

2. Where coaching takes place using a tape recorded performance. Once the trainees are familiar with using the tape their performance is not as inhibited as it can be with a coach sitting at their side – the pressure is less.

- the tape coaching session should be held away from the desk, preferably in a quiet and private environment;
- during the session the trainee should listen to his/her own performance and if needed go back over a point several times;
- the trainee should have control over the tape, allowing them to stop the tape at any time to clarify a point and provide explanation. This way they feel more in control of their performance and be more open to ways of improving;
- the coach can also focus in on more detailed points and if necessary either go backwards or forwards on the tape to reinforce a point. Also it is useful to be able to question such areas as 'what do you think the customer was feeling at this point?' or 'why do you feel the customer reacted in that way?'
- as with side by side training, at the end of each session summarise the trainee's overall performance then agree and write down the specific areas you wish the trainee to concentrate upon during the period leading to the next session. Ensure the trainee has a copy of these plans with targets and standards as appropriate.

SHORT- AND LONG-TERM TRAINING

Short-term training normally occurs as a concentrated activity, in the following situations:

1. *Induction*: New personnel naturally undergo a steep learning curve. It is important for them to gain knowledge of the company itself – its systems, procedures, personnel and even politics, the product or service portfolio, the customers, the competition and the marketplace. It is essential to plan in time for induction training – many people find it an inconvenience because it takes them away from 'other' work; however, conducted properly, induction training reduces or prevents the need for the new employee to continually disturb colleagues to ask questions on an ongoing basis.
2. *New products/services*: Technical or specification details of new products or services must be fully understood before people are comfortable to sell them. If not, they will stick to what they know – as we all do!
3. *New computer software/internal systems*: Once again, familiarisation with new systems is the quickest way to ensure competent and effective use. Making the time for this training is always a challenge but is worthwhile in the long term.
4. *One-off activities*: Telebusiness personnel sometimes work on exhibition stands, or attend calls with field sales personnel. They may visit a site to view their own products being used in a specific application and in all these instances, new or amended behaviours, skills and techniques are required. Planning in time to ensure the required knowledge can be imparted and acquired is vital.

Long-term training should occur automatically as part of the employee's relationship with the employing organisation. Every job should be a learning experience and the opportunity to develop in this way is highly motivational. Many companies still overlook this fact and hold the belief that if someone is doing the job they are paid to do to the required standard, then nothing else is required. Improved productivity comes from increased motivation. Increased motivation comes from creating new knowledge and opportunities to use that knowledge. An evaluation of long-term training possibilities is normally conducted during formal appraisal interviews, and it is heartening to know that in many large organisations, especially, increasing amounts of per-head annual training budgets are being set.

ASSESMENT CRITERIA

Many people ask me exactly what should and can be assessed during telephone dialogues. This of course depends upon the type of call – credit control, customer service, telesales? To identify a list of specific, measurable criteria is a discipline in itself, and training sessions for telebusiness personnel can also be constructed around these criteria. The following generic list might assist you to draw up your own:

- *Choice of words/vocabulary*
  Avoided use of relaxed words
  Dialogue using correct words
  No colloquialism/local phrases
  Minimised use of slang words
  Avoidance of confusing company jargon
  Used words matching marketplace
  Used words matching company image
  Used words to enhance product/service
  Minimised strong local accent
  Paused to add emphasis
  Repeated number/figure to confirm
  Sympathetic to foreign accents
  Recapped key points to confirm
  Remained calm/consistent/controlled
  Ensured no eating/drinking, etc.

- *Message taking/alternative*
  Explained reason for alternative
  Explained message, not negative
  Offered practical alternative
  Offered own name in full
  Offered first name only
  Stated relationship to person
  Stated department or section
  Stated job title
  Implied likelihood of assistance
  Displayed correct listening skills
  Confirmed understanding to contact
  Acknowledged points being offered
  Confirmed key points
  Recapped full message

Confirmed information written down
Correct methods of transferring data
Verbally committed next action

- *Signing off/finishes*
  Did not end call abruptly
  Did not hurry customer to finish
  Checked contact fully understood
  Checked no more information required
  Confirmed enquiry was complete
  Used contact's name to end dialogue
  Said 'thank you' to contact
  Said 'good-bye' and 'thank you'
  Avoided use of slang words
  Used appropriate sincere phrase
  Used corporate closing phrase
  Confirmed own name and telephone number
  Confirmed next action gained
  Gained commitment to next action
  Did not disconnect before customer

- *Transferring – making transfer*
  Explained reason for transfer
  Clarified benefit to caller, general
  Clarified benefit, correct name
  Clarified benefit, accurate solution
  Clarified benefit, not repeating
  Clarified benefit, saving time
  Clarified benefit, future reference
  Offered own name as fallback
  Stated where caller would speak to
  Stated to whom they would speak
  Avoided the word 'someone'
  Explained music on line
  Explained 'company information' on line
  Discussed with new client in-house
  Avoided personal bias/views etc.
  Offered alternative when necessary
  Requested that caller will wait
  Identified point of transfer
  Explained that line would go silent

- *Waiting/conversation*
  Explained reason for hold-up
  Described picture of situation
  Referred to support material
  Avoided phrases 'hold', 'hang'
  Used the word 'wait'
  Offered alternative to waiting
  Returned, explained further delay
  Used correct attention phrase.
  Used respondents name on return
  Apologised for delay
  Confirmed understanding of situation
  Recapped if call-back required
  Avoided talking across open line
  Used hold or silent facility
  Avoided using hold or silent facility
  Explained line would go silent
  Avoided hand over receiver
  Acknowledged cost in delay/relay

- *Mannerisms*
  Used proper stress and emphasis
  Did not argue/humiliate/patronise
  Smiled throughout the call
  Minimised any voice impediment
  Dealt with call concisely
  Moderated voice ensuring interest
  Varied tone as necessary
  Avoided hesitancy and was fluent
  Presented confident attitude
  Presented knowledgeable attitude
  Avoided negative image of company
  Maintained steady sequence
  Remained in control
  Attentive throughout dialogue
  Avoided talking over contact
  Avoided interrupting contact
  Confirmed understanding
  Remained calm, normal breathing
  Continuity noises
  Flexibility to customer's manner

VALUE-FOR-MONEY TRAINING

Training is still considered by many to be a cost rather than an investment. Whether it be external trainers such as myself who are 'bought in' for specified projects/periods, internal trainers who represent a salary, or merely the time implications of removing personnel from their normal workload and duties to attend training, if one assumes the quality provided is of the required standard, the expenditure – as with any other investment – can be justified.

Effective training enhances the knowledge, skills, attitudes and behaviour of the people, and hence their performance. The improved performance of individuals leads directly to profit. Such a payback can be rapid and significant, yet it is rarely measured or presented in financial terms. Perhaps it is because many managers cannot see the link between training and profit that a large percentage of organisations still spend little or no money on training.

Spending money satisfies an immediate need. Investing money provides the satisfaction and assurance of some future return. Training by its nature creates future benefits in terms of motivation, empowerment and managerial control. As with any other investment, two key elements must be quantified. The value and duration of the investment and the value and duration of the benefits received. Because the benefits will be received after the investment an estimate must be made; however, the difficulty of this calculation is present for any kind of investment, not just training. If an investment appraisal were to be completed for training projects, budget holders should take a more positive attitude to training investment and stop seeing it as an expense.

To effectively identify and quantify training benefits, it is necessary to know how the improvement of individual performance effects profits. For example, by increasing the quality and quantity of sales or reducing the quantity or value of the resources consumed. A training audit is the best procedure for identifying this. What is the current level of investment in training? Where is the investment directed? Where could training produce the greatest benefits? How can the training budget be redirected? Where should the training budget be increased? Neglected performance areas are those areas where the impact on profit can be clearly seen and which are not receiving effective training. Training which does not attack key performance areas, or cannot be seen to have an impact on profit, is misdirected even though it may be beneficial to the individual. An effective training audit will present a financial statement which will show the level of the present investment and its returns alongside the suggested level of investment and the potential returns.

HOW LONG SHOULD A CALL TAKE?

Today's computer software enables us to do many things which result in the ability to make or take more calls in an hour than ever before. The identity and telephone number of a caller can be made known to you as you answer a call. Screen scripts assist you in what to say, historical or financial information can be pulled from a database simultaneously, instructions to process an order actioned at the touch of a button. But this increase in quantity can pose serious dangers.

As a manager, it is important for you to decide how much you wish to utilise these features without jeapordising the quality of the call. What do we mean by quality? Let's take a situation where a potential customer has called your organisation to enquire about your product or service. They may require additional information to that which is featured in the brochure, they might be unclear of a particular aspect or feature of the product, or they may first wish to describe their own situation or circumstances before being asked questions or given information. Whilst effective marketing can identify groups of customers with similar needs, ultimately every customer is unique and wishes to be acknowledged and treated as an individual.

Much software still requires the telephone agent to ask certain questions in a particular order, and the effect of this could be irritating to the caller described above. Even software promoted as being 'totally flexible' does at some level condition the agent to conduct the call in a routine manner. This has an effect over time on how the agent *sounds*. Speech tends to speed up and whilst this on occasion can convey the impression of enthusiasm and efficiency, it can also make the caller feel rushed and overlooked as an individual. Management monitoring and repeated cautions through training are the key to preventing this unwelcome behaviour.

The quantity versus quality argument is particularly relevant in a telesales call. The techniques and rules of telephone selling (discussed in detail in Chapter 14) require the telesales person to:

1. *listen* for as long as is necessary so as to create in the caller the feeling and experience of being cared about;

2. *encourage* the caller to talk in detail about their problem such that the caller feels unhurried;
3. *ask* questions about the specific problem or requirement so that an impression of genuine concern is created;

and these approaches take time! Telesales people should therefore be judged on call content and outcome – not on call quantity. The analogy which springs to mind is attempting to fill a bath without putting the plug in. It is impossible to spend time on a call (quality) if one is constantly targeted on the number of calls taken or made (quantity).

MEETINGS

Someone once said, 'if it wasn't for meetings, we'd all be caught working!' Structured meetings with a meaningful purpose are vital, however meetings for meetings' sake are an abuse of time.

It is important to bring telebusiness personnel together for meetings as this is one of the factors which assists in developing team spirit. However, it can be difficult to arrange as the tendency – most especially with inbound call handlers – is to say, 'we can't take them off the phones just for a meeting!' Some creative thinking may be necessary. Is it possible to have a breakfast, lunch or even dinner meeting? These work well where team spirit is strong, although managers often have to overcome the initial reluctance to 'give up my own time'. Give them a reason to. Promote the individual and team benefits and/or reward them in some way for attending. Is it possible to gain telephone coverage from another department, the field sales team or even other managers? If the meeting only lasts an hour, the cooperation and willingness to assist will be greater. A one hour meeting is better than none at all. As people become used to meeting together, it is possible to cover more material in a shorter time.

Use this checklist of rules for conducting meetings to evaluate your own reality:

1. Apart from annual conferences or situations where people might have travelled long distances to attend, meetings should last no longer than one hour. People don't mind spending an hour and are far more positive about shorter meetings.
2. Every meeting should have an agenda. If possible the agenda should be circulated in advance of the meeting or even agreed at the conclusion of the previous meeting. Points raised which are not on

the agenda should be shelved for the next meeting. Circulating an agenda in advance, accompanied by an invitation to propose points to be included, helps to prevent this occurring.

3. 'Any other business' (AOB) should not appear on the agenda. It often does and is at the end which poses two problems. The unknown time content of additional points can cause a meeting to drag on. Secondly, very often people save their grievances for the AOB section. It is hardly positive for a meeting member to be storing up negativity! An acceptable amendment to the rule is to allow AOB to appear as the first agenda point. This at least gets rid of any negativity, and due to the main agenda awaiting, imposes a positive pressure to dispense with AOB as quickly as possible.

4. The amount of items on the agenda should be compatible with the time available and the number of people attending. Four agenda points can be dispensed with quite rapidly if six people are present, whereas if twenty participants wish to contribute to a point, proceedings take far longer. Better to have two one-hour meetings than one extended one.

5. Meetings should start on time even if some people are late. If you wait for the latecomers it gives them permission to be late again next time; it also tells those who bothered to be punctual their efforts were unrecognised – thus they might become a latecomer next time. Better to embarrass a few latecomers once in setting the precedent, than offend many others repeatedly with numerous late starts.

6. Each meeting should have a separate minute-taker and chairperson. It doesn't have to be the same people or the most senior person every time. Minutes should not be too lengthy, otherwise people don't bother to read them. Points of action along with dates and names is often all that is required.

7. If you are attending a meeting (as opposed to conducting one with your own team) it might be possible to delegate your attendance. This is a high responsibility motivator. Also, to save time, do you need to attend *all* of the meeting or could you leave when agenda points are not relevant to you?

8. Training should always appear on the agenda – a meeting is an ideal opportunity to develop and improve skills.

9. Sales meetings especially should be positive in content and must always end on a high note.

10. A small point which is often overlooked is the need to ensure no interruptions. Ask those present to switch off their mobile phones and arrange to have calls held. Most issues can wait an hour.

Below are some suggestions for agenda subjects at sales meetings:

1. Discussion of sales compared with targets;
2. How to attain more effective coverage of the territory/segment;
3. The need for selective selling;
4. Developing adequate customer records;
5. Selling the full range of products/services;
6. Professionalism in selling;
7. Good human relations in selling;
8. Overcoming customer objections;
9. Brainstorming for ideas;
10. Developing really good answers to commonly experienced objections;
11. How to 'sell' the company;
12. The sequence of a sales proposition;
13. How to get the customer's attention;
14. How interest can turn momentary attention into positive and lasting commitment;
15. How to be really convincing;
16. How to paint word pictures;
17. How to translate technical facts into reasons why the customer should buy;
18. How to develop and use case histories;
19. How sales fits into the marketing concept;
20. How to deal with the price objection;
21. How to sell quality;
22. How to sell effectively;
23. How to demonstrate a product/service skillfully;
24. Product/service knowledge quiz;
25. How to deal with paperwork;
26. Handling customers' complaints efficiently;
27. How to get the best out of current advertising;
28. How to present quotations;
29. How to use the telephone to obtain appointments at top level;
30. How to use the telephone as a sales tool;
31. How to obtain interviews from cold calls;
32. The use and misuse of our time;
33. Self-analysis;
34. Human relations in selling;
35. The best sales I have made this month;
36. The most difficult situation I have had to deal with this month;

37. The difference between our key products/services and those of competitors;
38. The biggest selling mistake I ever made;
39. The ingredients necessary for sales success;
40. Improving report writing;
41. Problem-solving;
42. Eliminating negative words and sentences;
43. The power of enthusiasm in selling;
44. Self-development;
45. Pre-planning;
46. How to use a diary to maximum effort;
47. Opening dormant accounts;
48. How to go after and open new accounts;
49. How to win a sales contest;
50. How to capitalise on the company's remuneration plan.

TIME MANAGEMENT

No management training course is complete without its section on time management because it is a fundamental skill. Organisations require people to do more and more in the same amount of hours. Personnel leave or are made redundant and are often not replaced. In a commercial sense, time has always been a budget item, however this fact does not automatically mean that managers know how to manage time effectively. Many still wrongly believe that time management is about doing things quickly. This is not the case. Doing things properly is the rule which doesn't always mean doing them quickly. Ensuring time is allocated and available to do things properly is the key.

There are many dimensions to time management. Below are some of the primary issues which affect telebusiness managers.

Understanding the Role and Responsibilities

A manager cannot begin to know where he or she is wasting time unless he first knows exactly what he is there for! What exactly are you paid to do? Could you answer that question now in one sentence?

What is the company's mission? What are the department's objectives? How are these objectives achieved through individual job performance? A detailed job description does ensure that personnel know precisely what is expected of them and, as covered previously, a defined performance standard leaves one in no doubt as to how the job needs to be performed so as to ensure the required result. A manager's job is to gain results through other people. Unfortunately, many managers do not do this because they:

1. have never been trained to manage and just don't know how to do it;
2. do not like managing and delegating so do the job themselves;
3. hold the incorrect belief that it is 'quicker to do the job myself';
4. feel threatened if someone can do a job as well as them so do not provide training;
5. simply enjoy doing the job themselves!

If the result is to achieve a certain objective, the method used is the manager's responsibility. If the method chosen is to do the job themselves rather than to gain the results through training and motivating others, the manager is clearly breaking the first rule of time management and heading down a slippery slope as well!

Using Fundamental Leadership Skills

Knowing and having the qualities of leadership, developing the team, planning and preparing, monitoring and controlling, attaining the required commercial and job-related abilities all combine to ensuring that a manager is able to maximise the use of time.

Analysing Time Wasters

A good place to start improving time management is to decide what is actually wasting your time. A simple method of setting priorities and deciding what to do when, first or next, is to list all your activities – all the things you actually do – and then categorise them as either reactive or proactive. Reactive is when you deal with issues which have been initiated by systems or other people and proactive is when you decide exactly what you are going to do and when you are going to do it. In short, reactive means no control, proactive means you are in control.

Next, identify what percentage of the time you are being proactive. The figure you should come up with is around 80 per cent. Managers who are proactive less than 70 per cent of their time are not managing! Now identify which of the reactive tasks can be refused or turned into proactive tasks. How many reactive tasks have you in fact *allowed* to disturb you – which in itself is a proactive decision. Often the key to eliminating or reducing reactive tasks is to become more assertive and decisive in your dealings with other people.

Setting Priorities

Review your list of tasks and activities. Then apply two words – urgent and important. Urgent and important when applied alongside what *you* are there to do. What you are paid to do. Your job. Which of the tasks are then urgent? Which are important? And which are both urgent *and* important? Most of the time, a task will be *only* urgent *or* important. About 20 per cent of the time, a task will be *both* urgent *and* important. These are the things we should do first. An example of a task which might be urgent but not important is producing a set of figures for a senior management meeting which has just been called for this afternoon. It is urgent of course, but as a telebusiness manager what is more important is your team and its workload. A situation which is important but not urgent is producing a competitor activity report. Very important when considering your responsibilities and the activities of your team, but not necessarily so urgent that it has to be completed by this afternoon.

It is sometimes useful to meet with the people with whom you have the most dealings and agree with them which issues are urgent and which are important so that everyone is clear and communication breakdowns don't occur out of misunderstandings. Some people use a 1–10 priority rating. Developing a common understanding is the most important thing. Use this rating to set your priorities.

Delegation

Delegation is a key management task and most relevant to effective time management. It does not mean, however, getting rid of all your work onto other people! You can delegate the responsibility of achieving a task to your team members, but you must retain accountability for their success or failure. Delegation is a process, and the following checklist may assist you in evaluating your own approach to the process:

- Analyse the task. Is it something which can actually be delegated?
- How does it have to be performed to be achieved?
- What are the time and resource constraints?
- Who is affected or needs to be informed about the activity?

- Who is to perform the task? Do they have the correct attitude?
- Do they have the time available given their own workload?
- Do they have the required ability? Now? or with training?
- Communicate what is required and train if necessary.
- Set time constraints.
- Monitor and evaluate.
- Act/assist/alter/ if necessary.
- Thank and praise the participant.

And don't forget – delegation does not always have to be 'downwards'. It can occur sideways or upwards in a traditional hierarchy.

UNDERSTANDING STRESS

Taking on too much work and not being able to keep promises and stick to deadlines can cause stress. Making a list of what is required to be completed quarterly, then broken down by month, week and day is an excellent way to plan. Reactive tasks can then be fitted in around proactive ones. Ensuring you have allocated sufficient time to complete a task is important when planning.

Interpersonal relationships can often be the cause of stress. Much time and personal energy is spent dwelling on negative relationship issues. We have all heard of 'psychosomatic illness' – where an individual believes (sees in their mind so clearly) that they have a particular disease and the force of their mental imagery actually brings on that disease. Medical research has shown that negative emotions have much the same effect on our body as psychosomatic programming. In fact, the millions of electrically charged cells in our body which promote health are deprived of that electrical charge when we indulge in negative emotions.

Much stress is generated because of long-held resentments or grudges relating to real or *imagined* upsets. Ways of releasing tensions resulting from these negative emotions are to:

1. Realise that whatever has happened in the past is *past* and *nothing* can change that;
2. Realise that holding on to a negative emotion harms only yourself;
3. Recognise that the relationship in which you experience the negative emotion is still very much alive – even though you may think it is dead – simply because it generates in you such strong emotion;

4. Visualise meeting the person:

   - speak your 'mind' openly and honestly,
   - imagine how they would see the situation which has caused the negative emotion,
   - discuss your and their viewpoints, trying as you do to genuinely understand the other person's point of view,
   - hear the other person say things that show they understand your point of view,
   - shake hands – see the other person express goodwill towards you.

5. Remember that psychologists say your dominant thoughts attract similar thoughts from others. So, if you hold in your mind a dominant thought of goodwill towards the person who has wronged you, that thought should magnetise some measure of goodwill from that person.

6. Identify your own stressors:

   - Feeling restless and unable to relax;
   - Being irritable and bad tempered;
   - Always feeling tired;
   - Difficulty in concentrating;
   - Loss of interest in homelife or hobbies;
   - Overworking;
   - Drinking and smoking more;
   - Losing perspective about the job and life in general.

However, every individual may suffer any of these symptoms from time to time without necessarily suffering from stress. If you are overweight, you may be feeling tired simply because you need to lose weight. Similarly, everyone has the odd day when they are irritable. However, if an individual regularly suffers from some of these symptoms and is unable to find a rational explanation, then he or she may well be the victim of stress.

Certain personalities are particularly likely to be affected by stress. Known as Type A, these potential stress victims thrive on competition and challenge, are aggressive and highly ambitious. They work excessively hard, are impatient and tend to be bad losers. They are frequently workaholics but are not necessarily high achievers nor even very efficient. The opposite is Type B. Such persons are balanced, likable, efficient and have no trouble in delegating. Type A is six times more likely to have a heart attack than Type B.

Personalities apart, other factors trigger stress. The working environment must be considered, for example too much noise, bad lighting and ventilation affect people. Too high a workload is obviously dangerous, and inefficient work makes staff feel insecure. Areas of responsibility are a major source of stress as are working relationships. It is also imperative that the organisation itself accepts that stress factors are inherent in today's working environment and that positive steps be taken to teach personnel to understand them on an individual and group level.

The golden rules for coping with stress are:

- Keep a sense of proportion;
- Give in occasionally;
- Go easy with criticism, you will only get it back;
- Take one thing at a time;
- Learn to delegate;
- Learn to ask for help;
- Learn to be assertive rather than aggressive or passive;
- Know how long you can concentrate without a break;
- Know when you are running out of energy and stop.

Annex A contains a paper on depression, written by a member of the Royal Pharmaceutical Society. Most people suffer depression at some stage in their lives and the paper gives realistic and practical information and guidelines as to how managers can assist staff with this affliction.

MANAGEMENT INFORMATION

As with customer information, details held regarding staff activity and performance is only meaningful if it can be analysed and used to take positive or corrective action. Cross-referencing of information allows management to see where there are gaps, who is doing what, and where people are working hard rather than smart. Many computer software packages are available for collecting and collating management information.

Historically, people were targeted on the number of calls made rather than quality of outcome. To some sales managers it didn't matter that an individual performing 10 calls a day was bringing in more first class, profitable business than his colleagues. What mattered was that his colleagues were making 50 calls a day! Deciding what to measure is of course the first step, and the telesales example below gives some ideas for monitoring options:

- Number of calls made/number of selling hours available;
- Targets in area/by quarter;
- Expense ratio/sales;
- Expense ratio/calls;
- Calls made/appointments arranged;
- Calls made/decision-makers contacted;
- Calls made/proposals (or quotes) produced;
- Calls made/products sold;
- Level of new business/existing business;
- Buying trends/industry;
- Length of sales cycle/per customer;
- Leads/sales conversion ratios;
- Proposal/order conversion ratios;
- Source of lead/business generated.

MENTORING

The principle of sharing skills and information between personnel – as opposed to continually relying upon the manager for training and guidance – is operated in the formal context of mentoring in many (normally large) organisations. Normally, a new employee or trainee is 'paired' with a more experienced member of staff with both structured and informal meetings occurring on a regular basis for a pre-determined period of time. Sometimes mentoring forms part of an employee development programme where the mentor works in a different department, often representing a new work area or position to which the individual aspires. Mentor reports then form part of any following promotional interview.

TRAINING SCHEMES

Many telebusiness positions do not require formal qualifications, and indeed the need for job-related knowledge is less pressurised with the advent of computer screen prompts housing extensive information. However, as part of the development and motivation of employees, many organisations are assisting and encouraging their staff to take National Vocational Qualifications (NVQs) and similar.

The National Council for Vocational Qualifications is a registered company established by the government aiming primarily to accredit

NVQs based upon the standards of competence at work, required by employers. This is attractive because it can be tailored, is realistic and rewards people who are highly skilled and experienced in a job but do not have any form of recognised academic qualification. Numerous NVQs exist and the units of competence required to achieve them are listed on the NCVQ database.

NVQs are issued by approved awarding bodies and reflect standards of work performance set by the relevant sector of industry and commerce. Routes for career progression are defined by the NVQ framework which divides into five levels of competence ranging from basic tasks at Level 1, through to senior occupational and professional skills at Level 5. The five NVQ levels – mainly assessed by observation in the workplace – are:

Level 1   Competence in the performance of routine work activities and/or achievement of a broad foundation of work competence as a basis for progression.

Level 2   Competence in a broader range of work activities involving greater individual responsibility.

Level 3   Competence in skilled activities which are complex and non-routine, including supervisory activities.

Level 4   Competence in the performance of complex, technical and specialised activities, including supervision and management.

Level 5   Competence in the pursuit of a senior occupation or profession including the ability to apply a significant range of fundamental principles and techniques. Extensive knowledge and understanding of the field and appropriate managerial capability are also involved.

NVQs are available for sales, marketing and customer service. The NCVQ is based at 222 Euston Road, London NW1.

City and Guilds offers over 500 work-related qualifications including NVQs and their own certificates. Both City and Guilds and the Chartered Institute of Marketing now also operate examinations in sales subjects.

EFFECTIVE COMMUNICATION

As a training consultant my time is often spent performing training needs analysis, interviewing staff prior to courses, and discovering issues which relate to work performance. The most common grievance I hear when speaking with telebusiness personnel – from all kinds of businesses – is that *'management don't understand!'*. This attitude and belief is sometimes ill-founded and sometimes unjustified. Either way, the feelings and views are real and must therefore be prevented at best and managed at worst. Left alone or more worryingly, undiscovered, they fester, multiply and eventually cause resistance, demotivation and average or below average performance.

Problems can be anything. Varying from poor support resources, unrealistic targets and inappropriate management style to pressure of workload, training deficit and historical cultures breeding blinkered thinking. The key issue throughout all these situations is the relief expressed at being able to confess to frustrations within the confidential framework of my interviews. Fear of reprisal, belief that 'it's not worth telling them – they won't listen', and no opportunity to express views are the three main contenders of poor communication.

A manager may be articulate, numerate, informed, well-organised, flexible, enthusiastic, professional, innovative and competent. But unless *effective* communication exists between managers and staff, the quest to head up a high performing, motivated and responsible team will remain nothing more than an elusive goal.

Understanding the day-to-day pressures, requirements, responsibilities and associated skills of telebusiness practitioners is investigated in Part III.

Part III
Practical Telebusiness and the Telemarketeer

8 Reactive or Proactive?

INBOUND OR OUTBOUND

Telephone calls are either taken (inbound/reactive) or made (outbound/proactive). Typically, in a sales sense, inbound calls comprise customer enquiries, leads from advertising, or freephone numbers and orders. Outbound calls comprise order-taking, lead and proposal progressing and appointment-making. Inbound and outbound calls can, however be of any nature ranging from cash collection to customer satisfaction surveys. Organisations with high volume 'traffic' often set up dedicated call centres with associated computer support, larger and well-known examples of these being banks, building societies and credit card companies.

When the telebusiness role or department is defined from the outset with clear instructions, job descriptions and definite management expectations, the function is normally carried out successfully. Problems arise, as in any department, when an existing role is to be changed or added to.

For example, in an attempt to improve customer service and increase sales, many organisations have strategically converted the *ad hoc* taking of orders reactively to a regular proactive service. Instead of the customer having to remember to order, calling at the last minute and wanting delivery of an order urgently, the supplying organisation removes this inconvenience by calling at a predetermined time and frequency. If correctly trained to administer this service, the supplying organisation can create additional business by briefing staff to use the telephone call as an opportunity to develop relationships, introduce special promotions, and increase order values or introduce new products and services.

Whilst this kind of change is born from sound commercial objectives, the effect upon people required to perform new ways of working and thinking can bring fear, resistance and demotivation. Alongside the logistical changes, taking time to address this issue through communication, training, example and counselling is very important. It is also fair and necessary. The classic example which I frequently experience is the customer service team who are **comfortable** giving information and being helpful, being asked to commence selling during an inbound or outbound call.

The telesales course I subsequently conduct has to concentrate far more upon attitudes than selling techniques. An individual who is by nature reactive, accommodating, passive and happy to **give** information is thrown totally out of their comfort zone when required to perform a proactive role and be more forceful, assertive, investigative and controlling. In essence, the person specification for a customer service position is completely different to that of a telesales person. Training in sales techniques is often not enough. The commitment seeker is normally a different person to the information giver.

AUDITING

In order to ascertain an objective evaluation of the true function, contribution and reality which operates in any telebusiness or sales office environment, it is beneficial to perform an audit of its operation. This assists in determining issues such as:

- Whether existing resources are being underutilised or overstretched;
- If workflow can be altered to accommodate new systems or practices with acceptable disruptions to customer service;
- How customer relations and sales opportunities can be improved;
- Where interdepartmental communications and interfaces can be enhanced;
- When new requirements can be handled as one-off projects;
- Whether a telesales function can be incorporated or should stand alone;
- If procedures are relevant, efficient and flexible.

The following questions should assist you in conducting your own audit:

General

Is the work of the sales department:

1. Up to date with

    - enquiries?
    - quotations?
    - order processing?
    - dispatch?
    - customer records?

2. Set out in the form of clearly written procedures?
3. Properly planned and supervised?
4. Effective in
   - guiding pricing?
   - controlling costs?
   - forecasting and controlling profits?
5. Organised to prepare reports to higher management for control purposes on
   - enquiries dealt with and outstanding?
   - quotations made and expected profit margins?
   - orders received and expected margins?
   - adjustments to order values and expected profits for extra work, changes requested by the customer, and/or losses due to omissions or decisions made by the company which are not chargeable to the customer?

Is the work-load of the department quantified and measured?

1. Is the average length of time taken to reply to routine letters and enquiries reasonable?
2. Is routine work properly planned, batched and controlled?
3. Is the department over- or under-staffed?

Do supervisors spend too much time on routine work instead of on supervision?

Is there effective control over the initial opening, marking up for action and distribution of sales correspondence?

Is there effective control over dealing with enquiries?

Is there an effective system for:

1. Dealing with telephone enquiries?
2. Taking action on customer complaints and analysing them?

Orders and Quotations

Is the price list revised regularly?

Are quotations prepared to facilitate cost control if an order is received?

1. Are costs detailed in such a way as to highlight variances from the original estimate indicating the area of responsibility for the

variances, for example sales, design, drawing office, manufacture, purchasing, erection and servicing?
2. Are adequate records kept of work undertaken that is extra to the specification quoted for the purpose of:

- updating cost estimates?
- ensuring that extras for which the customer is liable are properly charged to him?

3. Are facilities for proposal drawings readily available where required prior to quoting?
4. Are the estimators:

- competent?
- given adequate information?

Is there a clearly set out price and discount structure for each outlet?

Have prices been altered within the last three years?

Is the granting of discounts properly controlled?

Are the policies and procedures for credit control:

1. Clearly set out?
2. Satisfactory?
3. Properly adhered to?

- do the company's payments terms vary for different types of customers?
- is the value of outstanding debtors reasonable in relation to sales value?
- is greater effort required to collect cash promptly?

Is there an analysis of the size of orders to indicate whether the company is dealing with too many small orders which are uneconomic due to high selling and administrative costs for such orders?

1. Can the approximate cost of processing an order be calculated?
2. Could this be used as a basis for including the costs of order-handling in an estimate for pricing instead of recovering their costs as general overheads?
3. Is the minimum order level economic?
4. Should there be a surcharge on the price of small orders?

Is an integrated order/invoice/dispatch note system in use?

1. If not, is there scope for using such a system?
2. Are sales invoices dispatched promptly?
3. Is it clearly established as to how the company's terms of sale compare with those of competitors?

Is export documentation carried out by the sales office?

1. Is the JLCD 'Simpler' form in use?
2. Is the ECGD used to ensure against default in payment by overseas agent or customers?

Are improvements required in the records for:

1. Customer profiles?
2. Enquiries?
3. Quotations?
4. Customer orders?
5. Sales by product/service group, outlets, territories?
6. Orders received?
7. Outstanding?
8. Overdue?
9. Order trends?
10. Sales people's reports on calls?
11. Competitor's activities (including the keeping of an up-to-date intelligence library)?
12. Advertising and editorial enquiries?

Does each member of marketing and sales management know what information they require to assist them in carrying out their activities?

Does the accounts department:

1. Provide all the information which the marketing/sales department asks for at the time when it is wanted?
2. Provide an effective service to the marketing/sales department in appraising new service plans, budgeting, profit planning, interpreting results and suggesting improvements, and costing for pricing purposes in routine returns?

Does the sales office manager make adequate reports to higher management for control purposes?

Are outstanding orders continuously progressed so that any delays in dispatch are notified to customers before orders become overdue?

From an examination of the appropriate records and correspondence does it appear that:

1. Complaints are excessive?
2. Management deals with them satisfactorily?
3. Delays in dispatch are not notified to customers before they become overdue?

Are customers satisfied with the aftersales service given, particularly with regard to:

1. Speed of dealing with complaints?
2. Supply of spares?
3. Location of depots?
4. The application of guarantee work?

Is the market for spares and repair service being fully exploited by:

1. Informing customers of services provided?
2. Selling spares with new products?
3. Providing printed list of spares and their prices?
4. Are records maintained up-to-date of possible claims against the company arising from poor service?

Liaison with Production

Is production capacity:

1. Single shift worked?
2. Double shift worked?
3. Worked to maximum possible shifts?
4. Limited as to expansion?
5. Accurately assessed for forward loading?
6. Fully utilised?
7. Subject to seasonal fluctuation?
8. Geared to forecast turnover?

Does the company manufacture:

1. To order?
2. On sales forecast?
3. For stock?

Is delivery:

1. According to customers' optimum requirements?
2. Adhered to as promised to customers?
3. Properly controlled?
4. Change notified promptly by the works to the sales department?
5. Affected by the load on the design or drawing office?
6. Delayed because of customers' final agreement to specification?
7. Delayed by hold-up in sales office?

Are overdue orders:

1. Excessive?
2. Reported upon?
3. Affecting company's image and current rate of order taking?
4. Due to

   - inadequate or inaccurate information given to production by sales department or design?
   - delays in passing preparatory information to production from other departments concerned?
   - poor control of the supply of components and materials?
   - overloads in the sales department administration, design or production?
   - and if overloads apply,

     (a) is the overloading specific department known?
     (b) is the necessary action being taken to improve the planning and control systems, recruit staff, sub-control, or obtain improved or additional equipment?

5. Does the sales department:

   - take adequate interesting progressing orders?
   - inform customers of delays at the earliest possible opportunity?

Is the information on each sales order passed to:

1. Design?
2. Production in the form best suited for production purposes?

Is there sufficient liaison between the sales department and production controller, in contracting companies, between the person or section responsible for company contract coordination and all the contributing departments?

Sales forecasts:

1. Does the sales department give the production control department sales forecasts in the form required to plan production?
2. Does the production control department consider that the sales forecasts given

   - are in sufficient detail?
   - are reasonably firm?
   - are reasonably accurate?

3. In making the forecasts does the sales department:

   - distinguish between sales targets for salespeople and what they reasonably expect to sell, as set out in the sales budgets?
   - develop forecasts from trends of past sales?
   - take into account past errors in forecasting?
   - distinguish seasonal fluctuations accurately?
   - make due allowances for outside influences such as temporary government restrictions on spending and import restrictions, temperatures, weather?
   - take product/service lead times into proper account?
   - revise the forecasts at appropriate intervals?

4. Could sales forecasts be improved by any of the following methods:

   - analysing deviations from forecasts, for example by using exponential smoothing?
   - establishing the relationship between sales and external influence, for example using regression analysis or even simple graphs?
   - using moving averages for a specific period of time, say a month, derived from a number of past periods, say six months?

Where the company provides spares:

1. Are programmes of spares requirements provided?
2. Is the delivery position on spares satisfactory?
3. Is the method of inventory control satisfactory and adhered to?
4. Should there be a separate spares and service organisation

   - under the works,
   - under sales, or
   - independent?

5. Is there a repairs section in the works separate from product manufacture?
6. Is the pricing policy satisfactory from the point of view of

   - customers?
   - the company?

Do analyses of customers' correspondence and of cancelled orders and returns, indicate any marketing or production weaknesses?

Finished Goods

Is the trend of stock levels satisfactory in proportion to:

2. past sales?
2. forecast sales?

Does the responsibility for controlling the levels of finished stocks held for sale rest with:

1. The sales department? (it generally should)
2 The buying department?
3. The stock keeper?
4. A central stock controller?
5. Any other department?

Are finished product stocks held in more than one place?

Are the numbers of stock-outs for the last six months known?

Does an analysis of the frequency and reasons for stock-outs or lost orders indicate poor control of finished stock levels?

Is the re-order quantity calculated as frequently as the forecasts are revised?

In calculating the re-order quantity is account taken of:

1. Forecast demand?
2. Costs of carrying items in stock?
3. Costs of ordering and receiving items into stock?
4. Limits to the ordering capacity?
5. Limits to stockholding capacity?
6. Suppliers and manufacturers' lead times?

Is there any mechanism in the present system to enable the level of either the whole, or part, of the inventory to be increased or decreased easily and quickly?

In deciding when to place an order for finished stocks, are any of the following items taken into consideration:

1. Forecast sales during the suppliers' lead time?
2. Forecast sales during the review period?
3. Forecast sales during other periods which could delay the placing of an order?
4. Orders outstanding at the date of the review?
5. Future commitments, so far as they are not included in 1 and 2 above?
6. Safety stock?
7. Properly updated:

   - document processing lead times?
   - manufacturing lead times for assemblies, sub-assemblies and components?
   - purchase lead times for raw materials and bought-out components?

Is the re-order level calculated as frequently as the order quantity and revised forecasts?

If the present system purports to use minimum stock control level, does this represent:

1. The level at which a replenishment order is placed? or
2. The level below which the stock should not be allowed to fall?

Are safety stocks held?

Are stock levels reviewed frequently enough?

Are the stores well laid out and easily accessible, in particular for fast-moving items?

Are handling facilities satisfactory?

Are receipts matched with orders placed?

Is stocktaking carried out:

1. Continuously?
2. At the year end?
3. Periodically throughout the year?

Does the present system of coding provide a suitable classification of stores items?

Is control of stocks of finished products exercised in a manner which:

1. Meets customers' requirements satisfactorily?
2. Controls investment in stocks to economic levels?
3. Assists production to minimise manufacturing costs?

PROCEDURES

Creating change, introducing new working practices and enhancing old ones, involves procedures. Defining or redefining a telebusiness, telesales or telemarketing function involves procedures.

Procedures is a word which simply means 'the best way to deal with the objectives that are required'. In other words, a logical sequence of events, a system of working.

A company or department establishes its objectives.
Creates the procedures to achieved those objectives.
Designs the forms to control those procedures.

There are three rules to remember:

1. Departmental procedures must be coordinated.
2. Procedures must not demand more resources than those available.
3. Procedures must not become inflexible.

Criteria for determining what a new procedure should be, or for analysing the performance of an established procedure are the same:

- The human element.
- Effectiveness (including questions of time and speed).
- Cost (including labour, machines and resources).
- Flexibility.

There are four stages to consider when creating a new procedure (or examining an existing one):

Stage 1 (checklist)

1. Are there valid reasons to introduce, or change, procedures? (list the reasons).
2. Procedures must provide adequate management control.
3. There must be sympathetic consideration for those doing the work.
4. What patterns of work are likely, or have evolved?
5. What resources are available in labour, machines or office space? What is available on the market?
6. What computer/record systems have we got? How efficient are they?
7. Has the system any bottlenecks?
8. Will the new procedure create any bottlenecks?
9. How soon can I discuss with those involved in the department?
10. How soon can I discuss with other departmental managers?
11. Am I likely to get management approval?
12. What improvements should result?

Stage 2 (examine current procedures)

1. Collect all information:

    - Organisation charts;
    - Number of personnel involved and their personnel records;
    - Current job description;
    - Activity analysis of members of department;
    - Copies of all forms permanently in department, temporarily in department, created by and leaving department, created by other departments as a result of own department's actions.

And list:

- who uses them;
- how many they use;
- why they use them;
- how much the forms cost?
- how much time, on average, for each person to complete his/her operation.

2. Talk to the doers (get viewpoints on difficulty and/or frustrations).
3. Believe all that is told to you.
4. Write everything down.

Stage 3 (assemble current procedures)

Flow chart the forms:

1. Divide a large board (or paper) vertically into departments. Colour code and identify each.
2. Pin the forms in sequential order in each section. Use coloured ribbon (or pen) to identify how the form reached that department. Tag ribbon (or line) with label of average number raised per month. Every column in each form should carry a number in bold figures and the same number should appear on any form where the information repeats. Create an index showing how often each column appears on different forms, department by department and the totals.
3. Prepare a narrative step-by-step account of the total procedure, highlighting problems, or possible problems.
4. Create a chart of the operation performed in the procedure.

Stage 4 (analyse current procedure)

The analysis is conducted initially by yourself with your own notes on your own answers. The next step is to group the people involved and get them to analyse it also.

The basis of analysis and the moves towards an improved procedure are the simple questions:

HOW, WHY, WHEN, WHO, WHERE, WHAT?

For example:

Q. How do we know the customer's credit is OK?
A. By passing forms to accounts.
Q. What time is lost by passing forms?
A. About 24 hours.
Q. What percentage of forms passed to accounts result in credit not being sanctioned?
A. Less than 0.5 per cent.
Q. Could accounts notify the sales office weekly of bad debts?
A. Yes.
Q. Etc., etc.
A. Etc., etc.

If new (or revised) procedure seems an improvement, implement it. **Remember**, there is genius in simplicity and genius is 99 per cent sweat, and 1 per cent inspiration.

1. Take a step at a time.
2. Do not try to change everything at once.
3. Do not be frightened of making mistakes.

A MARKETING PLAN

Setting up a telebusiness unit or department with its associated personnel and resources ready and waiting to make or take telephone calls is not enough. Realistically speaking, this will only happen if it results from a sound business reason. This reason could be anything from the launch of a new product or service, the results of market analysis or the roll out of expansion plans. The size and operation of a dedicated, stand-alone telebusiness function needs to reflect some form of business or sales and marketing plan.

For readers who have not developed plans, the following guidelines should assist.

Business Plan

1. Market research.
2. Analysis of results.
3. Identification of goals.

4. Outline of strategies:

- short, medium and long-term objectives;
- marketing plan;
- budgets;
- research and development.

5. Implementation.
6. Evaluation and Control.

Marketing Plan

1. Market analysis:

- current market situation;
- background data;
- distribution;
- the competition.

2. Product analysis:

- summary of strengths, weaknesses, opportunities and threats;
- portfolio analysis (for example Boston matrix).

3. Intangibles analysis – evaluation of effect of issues over which you have no control, for example power of buyers and suppliers, legislation etc.
4. Define goals – objectives such as sales volume, market share, profit margins.
5. Strategy:

- market segmentation (customer size, buying criteria, customer industry);
- competitive positioning (high/low quality, high/low price, viz. competitors);
- product, price, place and promotion;
- define strategic or unique selling point;
- test marketing if necessary.

6. Action programme – implementation of strategies to answer what will be done, who will do it, when it will be done and how much it will cost.

The plan must be constantly evaluated and controlled because marketing is a continuous process.

FOLLOW THROUGH

The PC revolution and the advent of sophisticated databases has ensured that telemarketing is now a respected and strategic marketing tool. Even if computer software reminds you to do so, it is also a widely known fact that 80 per cent of sales opportunities are lost as a result of failure to follow up and follow through. In developing telebusiness activity specifically, the amount of work put in at strategic level, implemented at managerial level, and developed at practitioner levels goes to waste if follow-up is forgotten. In brief, money is lost. In addition, the improvements in customer focused marketing communications adopted by many companies still falls short of recognising the customer as *an individual*. Examples of this are too numerous to mention, however three personal experiences are worth particular note.

1. During my career, I have stayed in approximately 400 different hotels. Increasingly, customer satisfaction surveys by way of a card left in the bedroom are conducted. Many of the larger hotel groups despite subscribing to improvement programmes such as Investors in People (IIP) appear to be reducing their staff headcount, improving portion control and packaging guest self-sufficiency in carefully disguised customer charters. I have never once been contacted subsequent to being a hotel guest, either to be asked about my satisfaction levels, my future or individual requirements, nor the regularity with which I need to stay away from home. 400 nights at an approximate cost of £70 per night represents a revenue of £28 000 which would be substantially exceeded by the sleep-over requirements of large organisations. Lack of follow-through means no hotel or hotel group has ever encouraged my loyalty. An ideal opportunity to use proactive telemarketing.

2. A large computer consumables company placed a series of radio advertisements encouraging potential customers to telephone a central number to be put through to 'the store nearest to you'. I heard the advertisement on a Sunday and called the number on that same day. I heard a recorded message telling me that the store – albeit announced as local to me – was closed on Sunday. Apart from thinking the Sunday advert was a waste of money as the opportunity to take a spontaneous purchase from me had been missed, I experienced disappointment which would make me less inclined to remember to call the number on Monday or later in the week. Lack of follow-through caused lost business.

3. Whilst writing this book, I have also been attempting to buy a house. Whilst many people argue that houses sell themselves, because many properties are advertised through multiple not single agency, the quality of service does assist one when faced with a vast choice to decide whom to deal with and whom not. Not one of the numerous agencies with whom I spoke asked me more than two questions about my individual needs. 'What do you want to spend?' was the inevitable and in most instances only question I was asked. Similarly, whilst details of a particular property in which I had expressed interest were sent to me on most occasions, I was not automatically added to the mailing database and sent subsequent similar properties. I was forced to ring and asked for further information. In today's competitive markets we should strive to make it easy for the customer to buy. My personal house purchasing experience evidences again that lack of follow-through contributes to lost sales opportunities. An instance in which proactive telemarketing could have been used to secure competitive advantage.

9 Image Projection and Telephone Etiquette

BEING AN AMBASSADOR

The mark of how well an organisation communicates its objectives through management to staff is in how much responsibility is taken by an *individual* in performing their job. Sadly, the attitude of many customer service personnel is still 'it isn't really my problem'. As the link in every chain is equally important, so is every individual job function. Personnel who are proud of their role are a rarity. Those who are make excellent ambassadors.

Organisations spend vast amounts of money developing an image in the marketplace. This normally creates positive preconceived ideas and expectations which can be undone in a moment if the first conversation by telephone is poorly handled. This telephone contact could be described as a 'moment of truth'. The telephonist/receptionist in an organisation has more moments of truth with more customers in a day than any other member of the company. Measured this way, the telephonist is the most important person in the organisation. Telebusiness personnel claim a close second considering the volumes of telephone calls which are conducted with customers compared for example with the number of face-to-face calls which can be performed by field sales personnel. A mnemonic which assists in reminding the ambassador of the responsibility which all of us have when dealing with customers by telephone is:

C – comparison	Our customers compare us with the competition constantly.
A – advertising	Every member of the organisation should be aware of the image being created by advertising and other marketing communications, and should ensure the telephone manner adopted compliments that image.

R – recommendation   Many calls result from recommendation – the most powerful lead and opportunity to gain business. Don't waste these hidden chances.

E – experience   Previous experience of our product/service; different departments and individuals all create an expectation for the next-time encounter. Do you enhance or hinder future expectations?

TELEPHONE SERVICE

Some fundamental rules and techniques which assist us in ensuring we never deviate from the basic requirements of exemplary telephone behaviour are the following:

The Seven Rules for Dealing with Complaints

1. *Listen*: Keep quiet until the customer has finished. Let them get it all off their chest. Never interrupt.
2. *Empathise/apologise*: Always show empathy next. It is enough to say 'I'm so sorry you have had to call us about this'. If you know personally that it was your fault, apologise. Otherwise, beware of assuming the customers was right and your company was wrong.
3. *Reassure*
4. *Ask questions and record the answers*: What other details do you need to answer the problem?
5. *Keep the customer advised*: If you have to check up before you can tell the customer/caller what will happen, let them know when you will be getting in touch again with more information. Then keep your promise!
6. *Implement the action*: Put matters in hand, and follow up.
7. *Never, ever justify*: Explaining why it wasn't your fault does not appease the other party!

Message-Taking Rules

- *Why*: Explain why the message is necessary, use 'as'. Avoid: I'm afraid, I'm sorry, unfortunately, Oh dear, as openers!

- *Who*: Declare own identity by name/title/authority and relationship to required contact.
- *Take*: Full clear and accurate message to include caller's phone number and full name/dept./title etc.
- *Identify*: Own name/initials. Time/date message was taken.
- *Action*: Show clearly on message what action if any has so far been carried out.
- *Pause/leave*: Message immediately with required contact to avoid loss/delay/misunderstanding.

What is a Customer?

A customer is	A customer is	A customer is	A customer is	A customer is
The most important person that you ever contact in person, by mail, by telephone, or by any other means.	The purpose of your work. You are not doing him a favour by working for him. He is doing us a favour by dealing with you.	Not a cold statistic. He is a flesh and blood human being with feelings and emotions, biases and prejudices like our own	Not someone to argue with, or match wits with. Nobody ever won an argument with a customer.	A person who brings us his wants. It is our job to handle them profitably, to him and to ourselves for our mutual benefit.

That is what a customer is!

Always Use Questions During Telephone Dialogues

- Talking 'at' is just telling, and customer feels ignored.
- Talking 'with' is asking, and customer feels involved.

We should ask questions:

1. To gain information;
2. To give information;
3. To establish and then satisfy customer needs;
4. To draw out queries, fears and problems;

5. To refine buying objections;
6. To develop relationships and report;
7. To show interest in the customer, his business or organisation;
8. To help define route to sort out problems/complaints;
9. To speed up commitment;
10. To 'massage customer ego'!
11. To gain customers' opinion/views;
12. To save time with unnecessary 'waffle'!
13. To reduce expensive mistakes;
14. To keep call control;
15. To maintain customer loyalty;
16. To enhance company image.

Types of question to use:

1. Anticipated;
2. Open-ended;
3. Commitment/staircase;
4. Tie-downs.

Giving Numerate Information

1. When offering a series of numbers or items, tell caller at start of dialogue how many they need to listen for:

   - for example, 'there are four invoice numbers in dispute that need discussing'; or
   - 'can I confirm the six points highlighted in your recent proposal?' or
   - 'we have three new products which may interest you' or
   - 'there are five likely dates available to arrange a meeting before Easter'.

2. Give numbers in memorable chunks.
3. When giving telephone numbers, isolate the dialling code from main number with a definite pause – and tell caller which town the dialling code refers to:

   - for example, 'the number of our southern regional office is Reading – which is 01734 – pause –12345';
   - occasionally dialling codes differ from area to area.

4. Always repeat telephone numbers to avoid mistakes.

5. Avoid saying 'triple' when describing three consecutive numbers. For example, 333694 may be broken-down as 'three, double three, six, nine, four'.
6. When offering technical knowledge use 'simple' phrases/descriptions . Do not confuse with jargon or over-technical words.
7. Forty sounds like fourteen; nine sounds like five; 'spell' letters that could be confused such as g, e, b, c, also f and s.

Barriers to Communication

- Inability to see the object being talked about, unable to ask questions.
- No visual (non-verbal) signs.
- No clear reference points.
- Not enough time to prepare.
- Unavailability.
- Pressure of work – forgetting to pass messages on.
- Memory – not writing things down.
- Incorrect use of equipment.
- Language and dialect.
- Speed of talking.
- Jargon.
- Lack of interest.
- Noise.
- Lack of information.
- Priorities.
- Mechanical problems.
- Personality clash.
- Not willing to listen.
- Pre-conceived ideas.
- Feed-back confirmation.
- Lack of follow-up.

A KEY TO CUSTOMER LOYALTY

Losing a customer can be as traumatic in a commercial sense as breaking up with a partner or friend in a domestic or social sense!

If one evaluates the components of any strong personal relationship, it is soon evident that genuine concern and interest exist – if not mutual then certainly from one party to the other. From a verbal communication perspective, this manifests as a supportive, non-judgmental approach contained in an ongoing dialogue of questions. This applies equally in business relationships – the client becomes a firm friend. Experienced salespeople therefore learn to develop the skills of counselling as this ability is undoubtably a key to creating customer loyalty.

Definitions of counselling:

> Counselling involves giving time, attention and respect to another person. The task of counselling is to create an opportunity for the client to explore, discover and clarify ways of making resourceful decisions and gaining greater well-being.

> Counselling is a relationship. It involves a repertoire of communication skills, emphasises self-help and choice, focuses upon problem-solving and is a process.

> Counselling is not telling another person what to do or providing answers to problems. It is a process which enables the client to think differently about their problems, seek their own solutions and implement them successfully.

Figure 9.1 shows a systematic three-stage model derived from the work of Gerard Egan in *The Skilled Helper*.

Some counselling techniques and approaches are described in the following sections.

Proactive Skills

Opening Skills

- How do you see the problem? . . .
- Can you tell me the main difficulty with? . . .
- What is the biggest priority with? . . .

Continuing Skills

- And what problems did this bring next? . . .
- I can imagine how (time consuming). . .
- That's concerning, so what happens now? . . .

Stage	*Skills*

Stage 1 Exploration

The counsellor, by developing a warm relationship, enables the client to explore 'problems' from his or her frame of reference and then to focus upon specific concerns.

1. Attention giving
2. Listening
3. Active listening:

   - empathic understanding
   - non-critical acceptance
   - genuineness

4. Paraphrasing:

   - reflecting feelings
   - summarising
   - focusing, helping the client to be specific

Stage 2 New understanding

The client is helped to see him or herself and his or her situation in new perspectives and to focus on what he or she might do to resolve problems more effectively.

All the skills of stage 1, plus challenging skills:

1. Communicating deeper empathic understanding; 'hunches' and 'the music behind the words'
2. Helping the client to recognise themes, inconsistencies, etc.
3. Giving information
4. Sharing the salesperson's feelings, thoughts or experiences
5. 'You–me talk', immediacy
6. Goal setting/planning

Stage 3 Action

The client is helped to consider possible actions to take, evaluate the consequences, to plan, implement and evaluate.

All the skills of stages 1 and 2, plus

1. Creative thinking, brainstorming
2. Problem solving and decision-making
3. Using factual information to plan and evaluate

Source: Based on G. Egan, *The Skilled Helper*.

Figure 9.1   Three stages of counselling

Useful Feedback	*Futile feedback*
• Repeating key client words or phrases	• Ignoring key client words or phrases
• Reflecting client's feelings	• Telling client how/what they should feel
• Reflecting client thinking	• Telling client what they should think
• Reflecting what client is doing	• Telling client what they should do
• Reflecting how client is behaving	• Not acknowledging client behaviour
• Paraphrasing current thoughts and feelings of client	• Listing own priorities to exclusion of client's priorities
• Summarising client's views, feelings and actions	• Replacing or refusing to summarise client's views, feelings and actions
• Checking understanding of what client is saying, thinking, feeling	• Failing to check understanding
• Checking consequences for client of thoughts, feelings, actions	• Failing to check their understanding of consequences for client

Unhelpful Challenging	*Helpful Challenging*
• Forcing clients to face their concerns	• Inviting clients to clarify their problem
• Insisting clients do something else	• Asking how someone else would see their situation
• Telling the client there are no other choices	• Questioning which is the most important part of the problem which requires resolving
• Playing the expert	• Asking client for help
• Trying to be helpful too soon	• Waiting for appropriate moments
• Assuming you know how client thinks/feels about their choices	• Summarising how you feel/think about where clients are in their choosing
• Failing to check with client	• Encouraging client to doubt the current solutions

Reactive Skills

Facilitating Skills	*Blocking Skills*
● Checking that what clients say is what they really mean	● Putting own interpretation on what is being said – without checking
● Understanding the tone and mood of client statements, views, opinions	● Disregarding the tonality or mood of client statements, views, opinions
● Using and linking with client's use of language and spotting key phrases	● Using jargon which baffles client and ignoring or failing to use key phrases
● Hearing changes to client's emotions or moods	● 'Deaf' to changes in client's emotions or moods
● Attending to thoughts which matter to the client	● Directing clients to attend to what salesperson wants or thinks
● Discovering what clients make of their situation or what it means to them	● Telling clients what they should make of their situation or what it must mean to them
● Confirming with clients that you understand them	● Assuming you understand them
● Confirming with clients that they understand you	● Assuming clients understand you

Goals in Relationship Building

Counsellor Objective	*Desired Client Reaction*
● Establishing confidentiality	● Being satisfied with confidentiality
● Building trust and rapport	● Reciprocating trust and rapport
● Accessing relevant information	● Seeking information from salesperson
● Examining how client thinks, feels and behaves	● Discovering/improving own patterns
● Noticing what is important to the client	● Understanding what is important to self
● Focusing on client's needs	● Becoming more aware of own needs

- Reviewing past/present/future ways of satisfying needs and if they are being met

- Creating new choices with client
- Challenging client's beliefs
- Utilising client's resources
- Deciding desired outcomes and their implementation
- Maintaining client contact

- Engaging or participating with salesperson in reviewing ways own needs have been/are being met
- Considering new choices with salesperson
- Challenging own beliefs
- Releasing personal resources
- Considering/deciding/pursuing desired outcomes
- Wishing to maintain contact with salesperson

Much emphasis is placed upon the importance of customer service to influence the attitude of the customer; the concept of customer loyalty, on the other hand, requires an 'outside-in' focus that is geared more to behaviour than attitude. Customer loyalty is as, if not more, important than customer service, mainly because the cost of replacing a lost customer is five times greater than retaining one.

Four types of behaviour indicate customer loyalty:

1. Making repeat purchases;
2. Purchasing across product lines;
3. Giving referrals;
4. Demonstrating an immunity to the 'pull' of the competition.

Building a system and platform for customer loyalty requires organisa-tional planning across departments and functions; however, sales people can develop a customer loyalty 'index' themselves by asking what is creating loyalty to the company and what the company can do to increase and extend it.

Relationship quality plays a major role in the creation of customer loyalty, and transcends the conventional selling techniques. For example, recent research has concluded that trust is a significant factor in devel-oping and maintaining long-term relationships. Two salesperson attri-butes have also been identified as being relevant in affecting the relationship and decision-making process – *similarity* and *expertise*. Salespeople perceived as similar (that is in attitude, lifestyle or socio-economic status) to the customer are more likely to be successful in their dealings. Salespeople perceived as having expertise (not just product knowledge but market knowledge, application, logistics, environment and so on) is an important determinant of the customer's trust in the salesperson.

Long-term relationships can also benefit from the use of 'mutual disclosure' techniques initiated by the salesperson, and can create an atmosphere characterised by openness and candor which involves both leading and reciprocating customers' disclosures. In simple terms 'if I tell you something personal about me, you are more likely to tell me something personal about you.'

EXHIBITIONS

On occasions, telebusiness personnel are involved with face-to-face client contact at exhibitions. Here are some basic rules for exhibition attendance:

1. Invite your customers to visit your stand during your last or last-but-one call prior to the exhibition. The best time for invitations is from two to five weeks before the exhibition opens.
2. Tell your customers what new product/service will be on show and what special terms (if any) will be offered; also which of your top management members will be there.
3. Try to fix a date and time for each customer to visit the stand. Then the customer can be sure that the person they want to see will be present, and you have more assurance that the customer will actually come.
4. Bring a full set of sales documentation to the stand with you. Don't miss a single order for lack of paperwork.
5. Respect the rules and requirements of the stand-management. Arrive punctually in the morning and do not take more time off the stand than you need to. When leaving the stand, let somebody know where you are going and when you will be back.
6. Don't get into chatting groups with your colleagues on the stand. Keep a lookout for any visitors who look likely prospects for a sales talk.
7. Don't wear a new pair of shoes. When your feet begin to hurt, the smile on your face becomes forced.
8. If you are going to have a lengthy talk with a visitor, offer to accommodate their hat, coat, umbrella, briefcase and so on. They will then be better able to concentrate.

9. If you do not know a visitor, tell them your name, first name and job title. This is courteous and encourages the visitor to do likewise with you.

10. Try to judge whether visitors you do not know are just looking around or are potential customers. Ask factual questions, 'What are you using at present?' or 'How much do you produce daily?'

11. Don't address visitors with general phrases, 'Can I show you anything?', but specific phrases such as 'May I show you the new foot control 750kg press with automatic piston return?' People who are not interested will break-off the encounter.

12. Point out any new products/services – that's what customers have come to the exhibition to see. Moreover, new products/services are improvements on existing ones and anything the customer does not already know about is a new product/service to them.

13. Offer to give the customer full product/service demonstrations if they ask for them. Call in specialists who are present and give the customer whatever information they require.

14. Introduce your customers to the senior executive present, this makes the customer feel that they are taken seriously.

15. If another customer arrives while you are already talking to one, give them some product/service literature and samples. You must learn the difficult art of parallel servicing.

16. When you do not know a visitor, offer to send advertising material to their company or their private address. The advantages are that the visitor will not be forced to carry it; they will not dump it in a bin after leaving your stand, and you obtain their address.

17. Don't spend hours talking to very small customers and idlers. Close down unproductive conversations as soon as politeness permits. Your excuse is that you have other duties to perform.

18. Invite fault-finders or customers with complaints into a corner or inside the room 'to discuss the matter in comfort'. Don't let them sow doubts in the minds of onlookers.

19. Write down the main points of any important discussions: names, addresses, job titles, requirements, objections, agreements, dates, promises and proposals for further action.

20. At suitable intervals, take a snack (but not on the stand in full view of everybody). Purify your breath with pastilles or non-alcoholic drinks.

21. Tidy up the stand several times a day – empty ash trays, remove empty glasses, collect and arrange literature, tidy-up samples, re-arrange the furniture and pick up any paper from the floor.

22. Eating the wrong things can tire you. At midday you should have something that is low on fat, high on vitamins and not too much of it. Don't drink any alcohol but have a coffee afterwards.
23. Leave the lunch table in good time and take ten minutes walk in the open air. This will save you from feeling drowsy in the afternoon.

NO THANK YOU!

Many telephone dialogues occur as a result of direct letter or fax mailings. However keen our market research, segmented our data analysis, or individualised our communications, some people just do not wish to speak to us or receive documentation from us. The Mailing Preference Service, funded by direct-mail users and supported by the Post Office and data protection register, is a free opportunity for a consumer to decide whether or not to receive advertising mail. Completion of a simple form ensures your name will be removed from most mailing lists. For more information about this service, contact Mailing Preference Service, Department AM, Freepost 22, London W1E 7EZ.

NOT JUST A COMPUTER ENTRY

A paradox exists between the new drive in business to create loyalty and customer retention (as opposed to placing all efforts upon gaining new customers), and the impersonal effects of the new innovations in computer telephony. CLI (call line identification) identifies the number of an incoming caller and matches it to a database entry. This allows you to differentiate callers. If a caller matches the profile of a low-spend customer, they may have to experience sixteen rings before being answered by a voice response unit (computerised) whereas a caller identified as a high-spend major account will be answered in just three rings by a human voice! Whilst this may initially appear commercially sensible, there is one major flaw. The small-time spender may have a change in circumstances which automation cannot legislate for. The result could be a potentially large customer who defects due to feeling snubbed.

The management challenge and the practitioner's responsibility is to ensure all customers are given as personal service as is possible, so they are not made to feel like just an entry on someone's computer database.

10 Buying Behaviour

THE PARETO PRINCIPLE

The Pareto principle states that 80 per cent of any effort produces 20 per cent of the results, and vice versa. It is a natural law which can be applied to many situations. 20 per cent of a football team score 80 per cent of the goals, and vice versa. 20 per cent of our clothes we wear 80 per cent of the time, and vice versa. 20 per cent of a sales team produce 80 per cent of the orders, and vice versa. If we apply this rule to a customer base, then in most organisations we would discover that 20 per cent of the customers produce 80 per cent of the business, and 80 per cent of the customers produce 20 per cent of the business. In other words, most companies have a few major clients producing large amounts of revenue and numerous smaller clients producing small amounts of revenue. It should also follow that the large accounts bring in most of the profit although that is not always the case. Poor account management means that vast discounts, premium service and customer-led negotiations often erode profit margins.

In managing its customer base, the company through its sales personnel should attempt to do several things:

1. Identify why smaller accounts spend so little. Do they only have a small requirement which we fully supply or are they giving the rest of their business to our competitors – and if so, why? What can be done so that the account can be developed?
2. If the number of smaller accounts is vast and with no potential for development, is it wise for us to introduce a minimum order value or contract with agents and distributors to service the smaller accounts. At what spend level is it unprofitable to send an expensive resource such as a field sales person to visit these accounts? How would the relationship suffer, change or be enhanced *by telephone* – rather than field sales service?
3. Ensure the major accounts remain loyal to the company. Defection of a major account is costly!
4. Ensure the time spent maintaining major accounts and developing small accounts is appropriately balanced. Know where time should be

spent to develop commercial advantage and potential increases in business.

5. Calculate the amount of new business required to ensure over-reliance is not placed upon existing business to produce revenue. All companies lose customers through competitor activity, natural wastage and acquisitions so, over time, must be replaced. Ensure also that resources are adequate to cope with an intake of new business without diluting quality and service. Attempting to gain new customers when it becomes difficult to look after existing ones to the required standard is like trying to fill a bath without putting the plug in!

The Pareto principle reminds us that most organisations prefer not to 'put all their eggs in one basket'. Whilst long-term relationships, partnerships and consultative selling styles have become nineties business practice, over-reliance upon one supplier is risky. A Pareto evaluation of our customer base is a useful method of ensuring our sales plans accommodate normal buying behaviour. Many telesales personnel have no understanding whatsoever of what part their role plays in achieving the healthy balance of customers.

INTANGIBLE FACTORS

An intangible factor is something which although present, cannot be touched, viewed, heard or altered. In a sales sense an intangible factor is sufficiently strong as to represent 80 per cent of the reason why a sales is granted or refused. Tangible factors represent only 20 per cent of the reason why a sales is made or lost. Tangible factors are issues such as price, quality, quantity, delivery and availability – all of which, given the appropriate authority or alteration of specification, can be altered.

Whilst intangible factors are never seen on an order form nor disclosed during a telephone call, given their significant contributions to the sales dialogue we will examine them from four perspectives – those which influence the customer, the salesperson, the supplier and the product or service itself.

Customer

Loyalty, habit, historical relationship, prejudice, sentiment, apathy, laziness, reluctance to change, fear of change, pride, ego, flattery, attention to personal needs, personal relationship, trust, rapport, attitude, surplus money in budget, confidence – in equipment and supplier, means of gaining esteem with his/her company, pride of possession, prestige value, apparent value for money, feeling of 'a good deal' – gain, ease of justification of purchase, personal pressures at time of decision, impulse, demonstration of decision-making power, security, peace of mind, satisfaction of emotion, company policy, politics, national attitudes, local loyalty, spreading risk, speculation, anticipation, relative status compared with other customers, social implications of purchase, recommendation from others.

Salesperson

Personal presentation and acceptability, personality, credibility and reliability, enthusiasm, personal relationship, trust, rapport, attitude, empathy, identification with customer's needs, communications, ease of dealing, timing, 'technical' competence, integrity, trust.

Supplier

Image, reputation, prestige, stability, politics, national attitudes, company policy, location, identification with customer's needs, resources, record as an employer, social acceptability, 'technical' competence, back-up facilities.

The Product or Service

Presentation, reliability, image, implications of design, identification with supplier's needs, manufacturer's resources, technology, safety.

Being *aware* of both the positive and negative effects of intangible factors will ensure we listen more carefully during telephone conversations. What we then have the power to change is *our* approaches and responses.

BUSINESS TO BUSINESS

Telemarketing and telesales in industry and general business is quite different to consumer sales and marketing (individuals or families). The buying situations in the two areas are different, with special problems requiring individual responses by companies selling into them. It is vital that this background information is understood by telebusiness personnel who wish to become more 'commercially aware'.

Capital goods and service contracts are generally purchased infrequently and require a large commitment to expenditure. This highlights some radical differences in industrial marketing:

1. The small scale of purchase in consumer goods means that the customers cannot be treated individually, and with self-service shopping, they buy without face-to-face contact with either the manufacturer or retailer (hence the scale of consumer advertising).
2. Where capital goods are concerned each customer is given individual attention, and in many cases the product can be modified to match the customer's specifications. Hence, the sales-force is the dominant part of the marketing strategy.
3. The number of customers differs enormously; compare for example the number of customers for a breakfast cereal and the number of outlets that will be required to stock the item, compared with industrial customers and their distribution channel. In the latter, it is quite common for the distribution of the product to be supplied direct from the manufacturer.
4. Capital goods are more susceptible to cyclical patterns. Assuming an average five-year cycle, with a three-year lead time to bring extra capacity into production, then the manufacturer will be required to invest in 'lean' times during which cash flow may curtail expenditure.
5. Most buying for industry is for technical products which are evaluated technically by the buyer. This is not the case in the consumer marketplace.
6. Purchasing motives are also different. Most buying decisions in industry are to fulfill organisational goals, for example to cut costs, increase output and so forth. Industry doesn't often buy to impress friends, but as we learned about intangible factors it is wrong to suggest that the motives for industrial purchase are less complex than for the consumer market.
7. Organisations do not set goals, nor do they make decisions – **people** do. There are more people involved in the industrial buying process, all of whom have different perceptions of the nature of the problem.

CONDITIONS AND INFLUENCES

The general business cycle is a well-established phenomenon. Cash flow is related to the cycle, and every long-term capital project commitment can be seriously hampered by even short-term weak phases in the cycle. Industrial confidence swings with general business conditions, optimism leads to new orders, pessimism to cancellations or postponements. Companies selling to industry, therefore, need to predict trends in business conditions.

The structure and style of an organisation conditions much of what goes on within it. First the degree of centralisation can shape the purchasing procedure. Highly centralised organisations leave little discretion to operating branches. They may have fixed policies which mean that all purchases above a certain sum need central approval. They may also have a central list of approved suppliers, and a highly systematic purchasing procedure. Quite small detail may be required on the authorisation documentation. However, all this may be totally different in a decentralised structure.

It is essential therefore to first 'know your customer' – this could be several people at a branch and several people in head office. More importantly, it is essential to know the organisation's rules and procedures. Successful telebusiness people will hope to find out as much about the paperwork involved as members of the buying organisation. Ideally, the selling company will know the buying organisation's structure, the relationship between divisions, key purchasing procedures, and the important people involved.

It is also important to seek out the DMU (decision-making unit). For small purchases it might be just one or two individuals, for large capital items it might be numerous layers of operatives, management and directors. One also has to gather specific information on the relative strengths of DMU members, their individual sets of evaluation criteria, their perceptions of the problem, and some indication of the conflict resolution procedure employed.

While the firm may employ outside researchers to gather this information, many companies see this as an important function of the sales-force. It is the sales team that is in constant contact with customers (actual and potential), and they will need and use most of the information regarding DMUs. For this reason industrial salespeople are generally expected to make comparatively fewer calls per day than a consumer telesales representative.

It is the telesalesperson's responsibility to keep comprehensive records of DMU membership, motives and relationships, and to have knowledge of organisational influences mentioned earlier. In addition, they should also be monitoring their customers in terms of the stage reached in the buying process.

There are considered to be three main 'buy classes':

- *New task*: No previous experience with the product category.
- *Modified rebuy*: Some change in choice criteria.
- *Straight rebuy*: Well-established choice criteria and brand education.

In the new task situation, the purchasing company will go through all the buying sequence. In the modified rebuy, only changes are being made to the specifications and there may be a little research involved. In the straight rebuy it is quite common for no research to be undertaken as an order is routinely placed. The DMU's role will vary from very active in the new task phase, to dormant in a straight rebuy

As mentioned earlier, it is people not organisations that make decisions. Individual factors, therefore, present another influence on the buying decision. One element in this will be the acceptance and interpretation of information. It must be remembered, however, that perception is subjective. Now another element has to be added – the concept of source credibility. 'Who you are does affect how buyers react to what you say.' High reputations make access into prospects easier, and assist in an initially favourable reception. The nature of the sales presentation also has a marked effect, thus the fundamental principle of commercial awareness and personal credibility conveyed through voice tones and intonations is of paramount importance.

COMPETITOR ANALYSIS

It is widely recognised that there are only five main criteria for buying. Price (what is paid, discounts, credit terms), quality (of product or service, technical support, training), quantity (volume, specification), availability/delivery (when, how often or flexible) and service (presales, during supply and post sales). The key is to identify what each of these five mean in your own business. Then tailor your telephone dialogues around identifying the customer's views and desires related to the five criteria.

Your organisation will be promoting a unique selling point which sets itself apart from competitors, but when evaluating the five criteria and comparing it to your competitors, in the final analysis you will find very little difference. Companies cannot afford to be too different in a competitive marketplace. It is, however, important to be aware of the differences and the features within the competition. A buyer or decision-making unit are sure to investigate different suppliers so to conduct an informed and confident conversation, a telebusiness agent must be equally informed.

Read the papers, subscribe to and read relevant trade journals, call up and attempt to gain brochures from the competition. Go to the reference library and obtain company details, and make your own judgments regarding service levels by speaking with their sales people. Draw up a comparison chart of your features and criteria compared to theirs and have it handy as a pop-up screen on the computer, or as a hard copy single A4 sheet for quick reference. If you don't, your counterpart in the competition will!

11 Scripts and Other Things

TO SCRIPT OR NOT TO SCRIPT?

Stereotypical scripts are those we have experienced when being used by the unfortunately notorious double-glazing telesales person. Stilted questions and robotic responses used in this way approach contact with potential customers as nothing more than a numbers game. Throw enough mud against the wall and some of it will stick! Whilst this approach is still used by some, the days of unqualified mass contact are being replaced with more selective, market-segmented methods. A set of structured, scripted questions asked of an existing customer at the end of an order-taking call, to introduce a new product or entice purchase of an associated or additional line, can be very successful.

But scripting, as now defined and available within computer software packages, is vastly different and has applications which were never appropriate with more historical methods. The flexibility of these packages by utilising 'branching' screen prompts, enables the call to be dealt with in a natural and spontaneous fashion within less obvious control parameters but still leading towards the desired outcome – be it an appointment, a brochure or an order form.

Scripts can be written to cover all relevant information and provision made for data entry in no specific order, thus eliminating the impression of staccato 'question and answer'. Scripts can be designed to cover every possible response, branching according to the designed objectives of the conversation and containing answers to possible objections. Most computer scripting packages also have provision to allow for associated activities to be automated and many can be integrated with existing systems such as your database. Knowledge-based or 'expert' systems allow non-specialised staff to interrogate vast amounts of information quickly and accurately.

Campaign-targeting, screening, recruitment response, data capture and analysis, customer satisfaction levels and staff motivation should all improve through the use of effective scripting and administration; paperwork, the need for training, and time spent on calls should all be reduced with the right package. The wrong package, that is one which is essentially inflexible, can have disastrous results not dissimilar to the reaction caused when using the old fashioned scripts!

HOMEWORKING

There is a growing trend in business to use consultants and contractors – as opposed to fully employed personnel – who work from home and thus do not require company-funded heat and light around their desk in the office, and in the main are responsible for paying their own tax and insurance. The computer industry is a typical example. It uses more contractors than employed staff. Some banks have taken the step to allow staff to work from home thus saving costs and facilitating more flexible working hours. The same applies to telebusiness. According to BT research, 28 per cent of companies now have employees who work from home. With the use of networks and modem links, the telemarketeer or telesales person can physically work from home but still access the resources and information based in a central office which are required to be effective. One of the many benefits is the reduction in call costs if the homeworker is briefed to contact customers and potential customers locally. The individual can still attend the office for meetings if required, but an essential recruitment criteria for the person specification is the self-discipline and enjoyment to work alone.

WRITTEN COMMUNICATION

Once again, advances in information technology allow us to produce highly relevant and personalised letters, proposals and bulletins. But whether it is the next mailshot or the internal newsletter, a first-time write has to be compiled by someone. It could be argued that people are no longer stretched in that 'someone else' and then the computer obviate the need to construct language. (In fact, many people believe there will eventually come a time when children will no longer need to learn to read and write as learning will be screen based, multimedia and virtual-reality driven!) But in the constant drive to maximise time and resources, 'one person for the job' is an inevitable benefit.

If you don't have the benefit of an expert or automation, the following basic guidelines may assist:

Letters

Using a very simple principle, we will take a look at how to put together good letters that 'get the message across', support the company image and avoid pitfalls.

- *Situation*:   This is quite a simple statement of factors or facts about the current or past position.
- *Complication*:   This is a development of the facts stated in the situation. It poses a problem, if indeed there is a problem present, and asks a question.
- *Resolution*:   How do you intend to resolve the matter? – that is provide a solution to the problem.
- *Action*:   This is quite simply the letter-writer saying, 'We know the problem and this is how we would like to solve it. Accordingly, we have taken "this" and "that" action'.
- *Politeness*:   This hardly needs a comment, save to say that good human relationships are vital in both business and private life. You are more likely to get a good reception to your letter if you conclude with an expression of good will.

Business letters should be simple, clear and to the point. Stick to simple words, short sentences and clearly defined paragraphs. A letter is a written message from one person to another. It communicates to the reader the facts of the message plus an impression of the writer and the organisation for which he/she works. Often the impression gained is different from that intended; the writer (and his/her company) can convey his message in a muddled and confusing manner.

1. *Decide what to say*:   Make sure you know what you are going to say, before you decide how you are going to say it. When it is clear in your mind, write down all the points in the form of a plan or notes.
2. *Put it in sequence*:   Put your ideas in a logical sequence. This prevents you from jerking from one point to another and back again. An ordered logical sequence of points will carry your reader's understanding through the letter, step by step.
3. *A paragraph for each step*:   A letter without paragraphs can be difficult to understand and depressing to read. Each subject should be given a separate paragraph. This helps the reader to understand you and to progress from one step to another.
4. *Immediately identify the subject*:   Make sure that your reader knows exactly what the letter is about. One way to do this is by giving the

letter a heading right from the outset. The subject is immediately identified and the reader knows right away what the letter is all about.

5. *End by pointing the way ahead*: End your letter by pointing the way ahead. Never leave the reader wondering what the next move is, or who takes it. Make a positive statement about what you want done or what your intentions are.

A good letter written to the five rules can still be a failure if the following points are ignored:

6. *Use short simple sentences*: Short simple sentences are easier to understand than long complicated ones. Aim for fifteen to twenty words to a sentence, and five sentences to a paragraph.
7. *Use punctuation to help understanding*: Punctuation should ensure that the message is understood. What pauses and inflections do for speech, punctuation marks do for writing.
8. *Use simple words and few of them*: Avoid using business jargon, artificial words or long-winded ways of saying things. They are **your** thoughts, put them into **your own words**.

Queries and Complaints

It is often difficult – and pointless – to distinguish between queries and complaints. A query mishandled instantly turns into a complaint, a complaint skillfully used can turn into a query, and even into an enquiry or order.

1. *Find exact nature of query*: It often happens to all of us that we answer the query that we think was raised. A telephone call, a letter or a visit by a salesperson might often be well-worthwhile.
2. *Check your facts*: Often you will need to get information from other branches depots, departments or even just check your own files. If this will create a delay, write a brief letter saying you are sorry he is distressed, but admit nothing. Write 'Thank you for bringing this to our notice'.
3. *Get action*: Most queries want action – even giving information is a form of action. Make sure the action happens. 'It is still with our department' pleases very few people. It is up to you to get action for your customers.
4. *Tell the customer*: It is the customer's right to know what you have done or found out for him. (It might be useful sometimes to have this letter delivered by hand by the salesperson.)

Direct Mail Tips

1. Above all – is the offer clearly and easily understood?
2. Does the mailing talk too much about the product/service, too little about the benefits?
3. Is there a deal – a discount or premium that enhances the attractiveness of the offer?
4. Does the copy contain big ideas?
5. Is it easy for the prospect to order?
6. Is the mailing dramatic?
7. Is it totally believable – does it inspire confidence?
8. Does the outer envelope persuade – or provoke – the prospect to open it?
9. Is the letter copy personal – written from one person to another?
10. Are the transitions natural (does the copy flow smoothly)?
11. Is the copy written in clear, concise language?
12. Do the graphics help – or get in the way of – the message?
13. Is readable type used in the mailing?
14. Is every relevant selling benefit explored?
15. Does the copy repeat the key selling points?
16. Does the mailing exercise subtle flattery?
17. Is the guarantee of satisfaction strongly emphasised?
18. Does the mailing sustain the big idea at the end?
19. Does the copy provide solid reasons for ordering now?
20. Above all – is the offer clearly and easily understood?

DEBT COLLECTION

Debt Collection is about collecting money that is rightfully yours; it should be easy. However, the reality is that it is a very difficult, time-consuming exercise.

Collection of money owed to you can threaten the very survival of your company. Every company needs cash. You can have healthy orders booked, thousands invested in assets and still go out of business. Cash flow is vital, and one of the main contributing factors to good cash flow is the speedy collection of money owed to you. An overdue account is a free loan to the customer. So why should the customer pay quickly if you are providing cheap finance and are easily put off collecting. With all this hassle why don't we just forget the one or two bad debts. Surely it would be cheaper just to walk away and get on with the business of dealing with the paying customers. Not so. How long do you think it would take to make up a bad debt of say, £400? Would it just mean the sale of a few more items around that price? No!

If your company worked on just a five per cent profit margin you would need to sell at least £8000 worth of product to cover a £400 loss. Here's how I came up with the £8000:

$$\frac{\text{Bad Debt} \times 100}{\text{Profit Margin (\%)}} = \frac{\text{Amount of product need to be sold to}}{\text{recover the bad debt}}$$

This is why we must recover as many bad debts as possible!

Call preparation is vitally important. Checking the debtor's history, details, terms agreed, your own call objectives and how you will answer likely objections are all necessary before you pick up the telephone. During the call you should consider the following areas:

- *Presenting a professional image*: It is important to place yourself in the right frame of mind. You must at all times present a professional image if you want the debtor to respect your needs and wishes. The first impression at the start of the call will set the scene and show by the tone of voice the firmness and dedication to gain commitment of the overdue debt. So voice projection, tone and emphasis must be correct and reflect the company's image and attitude towards the debt. Sounding casual can sound too familiar and dilute the firm professionalism required.
- *Using effective communication skills*: The incorrect use of the telephone can not only prevent good communications but may also leave people with a totally wrong impression of the caller and his company. It is worthwhile remembering that the image you project on the phone influences the way people think of your entire company. You are the company – good or bad! So make sure that your telephone manner is a company asset not a business liability.

Next be careful of how to speak. If you mumble or speak too fast or too loud then you're actually creating a barrier between yourself and the person on the other end of the line. Remember that the only point of contact between the two of you is by voice. If yours can't be clearly and easily understood then you're defeating the object of every telephone conversation that has ever been made. It is worth remembering that in using the telephone we must rely solely on our voice to get our message across. It is better to slow down and get one idea across than to try and cram three of four ideas into the same time scale, and miss out on them all. You may think that you've got the three ideas across but will the debtor stop you and ask you to explain? Unlikely.

So speed is one problem; another is *mumbling*. We need to speak clearly and distinctly but avoid over compensating by shouting and committing grievous bodily harm to the inner ear of our poor debtor. Ensuring we modulate voice tones so as to sound interesting is also important. Before you make a call take a moment to shrug off any bad humour. Your telephone voice must sound friendly no matter how foul a mood you're really in – don't let it show in your voice. A good telephone manner could be described as relaxed, friendly, positive and helpful. When you're talking avoid one word responses like *yes*, *no*, *why* or *when* – it makes you sound abrupt and disinterested as if you can't wait to get off that phone. Don't be abrupt – keep it brief and to the point.

Be clear on how to approach the decision-maker – surname, title, first name, etc., and be sure the contact is the correct person with whom you plan to establish a dialogue. For example, a small family business might often have a number of people with the same surname.

Making an early morning call at the very start of their working day shows how seriously the situation is taken and it gives the customer all day to send in the cheque or see to the query which has caused the delay in payment. At no time should the decision-maker be left alone over the phone. Have all necessary paperwork available on the desk. If you leave the contact alone while you go off to check up on information, they may think up extra excuses, or worse, 'hang up'!

In order to get the debtor to commit to payment you must first develop dialogue. Mention the exact amount of the debt at the start of the dialogue and again during the call. Then again at the end of the call when confirming the amount promised. Remember not to answer your own questions. During the dialogue the use of well-timed and planned questions is essential; it implies strength, confirms actions, builds good customer rapport and draws out problems and queries that need prompt attention to prevent further payment delays.

Remember customers rely on put-off excuses and non-payment objections to delay settlement, and the professional collector must be ready to handle these with confidence.

12 Telesales

HOW TO SELL

It doesn't matter whether you sell a tangible product or an intangible service – or whether you sell something worth a hundred pounds or a hundred thousand pounds, the common thing for all sales people is the need to encourage another human being to make a decision in their favour. Selling is presenting in a manner which people find acceptable, so that they decide to buy. Consider the word 'presenting' – it applies to the company and the product but primarily to the salesperson. One thing for certain is that people buy people before they buy products or services.

I was involved in some research that was conducted with some high-achieving sales people who were earning in excess of a hundred thousand pounds a year, and we interviewed them to discover what they were doing that the rest of us weren't! The main thing was their ability to present in a manner that the buyer found acceptable. We all sell as an extension of our personality and therefore we're comfortable with our selling approach. But is the other person? For example, if you're a natural extrovert it would follow that you are comfortable being very verbal, and if the buyer is quiet and a listener your verbal sales approach would be acceptable to the buyer. But what if the buyer was also a verbal type and liked the salesperson to do a lot of listening. Shutting up and listening wouldn't be so comfortable to an extrovert salesperson, but if they didn't do it they wouldn't be presenting in a manner acceptable to the buyer! And vice versa. The ability to listen and identify the style of approach acceptable to each individual buyer was a definite skill owned by this élite bunch.

It might be useful to evaluate some of the other criteria which resulted from the superstars research – which incidentally involved salespeople from many different types of business and industry. There were five main skills which the high achievers had in common:

- First was self-organisation; knowing the difference between being busy and being effective.
- Second came the ability to identify the real and true buying criteria.

179

- Third was the judgment ability to identify potential before committing effort.
- Fourth was the use of analysis and perspective to identify winning trends.
- Fifth, and finally, the ability to persuade, control and convince groups of people.

Interestingly, vast product knowledge was not present with many of them, and business skills featured as having the same if not more importance than closing skills.

Selling is quite a natural process and it is only the techniques we apply which affect the outcome or direction of this process. The first stage is that of planning and preparation. Of course as with many things in life, the preparation stage plays a major part in whether the outcome is successful or not. Next it depends on what type of call you're making. Is it a cold call, a service call or perhaps a call to follow up a proposal? A fundamental question to be considered is whether or not you are talking to the right person or people. In other words, those who would be in a position to make a decision in your favour.

There are two mnemonics which a lot of people use to help themselves do this. The first is MAN, which stands for Money, Authority and Need. In other words, the three things that the other person must have before you will spend your valuable time doing business with them. Are the finances available, who signs the cheques and does a requirement exist? The second mnemonic which links closely with it is DMU – Decision Making Unit. In many organisations these days more than one person will comprise the MAN. Clever buying is undoubtedly another way to make money and the buying responsibility has widened out considerably. A lot of sales people have been caught out by spending time with just one person in an organisation to find at the point of closing the sale that the individual they've been spending a lot of time speaking to is not the sole decision-maker.

BUYING CRITERIA

Next it may help you if we look at the main criteria involved in buying. Now a lot of salespeople say to me on courses that 'our business is different . . .' in fact I'd be retired if I had only 10 pence for every time someone said that to me! But the common thing we are dealing with is people. And believe it or not, there are only five criteria which people seek irrespective of the product or service – they are:

- price,
- quality,
- quantity,
- service, and
- availability (if you sell a service), or delivery if you sell a product.

What it is important to do is identify what those five things mean in your business.

Quality in the pharmaceutical industry for example means that the drug works without any side effects, in the travel agency business that holiday flights depart on time and for the construction company that potholes don't appear in the road prematurely! Quantity for the pharmaceutical company would mean whether a particular drug would come in inhaler form as well as tablet form, for the travel agent whether the short breaks were available with departure seven days of the week, and for the construction company whether a mini-digger could be provided instead of, or in addition to, a JCB.

Availability for the drug company would be whether a bottle of 500 pills and not just 100 could be delivered today, the travel agent whether sufficient seats were available on one flight, and for the construction company whether the required amount of equipment was available for building in more than three counties in one day. Price in all instances is what must be paid in return for supply, and service would cover everything from extended warranty, stockholding, free training, loss leaders, credit terms, technical service, to maintenance credit terms and financing.

A question I would ask people on courses is 'which one is the most important in your business?' Let me ask you the same question . . . well the correct answer is that irrespective of the business you are in, one is not more important than another. Why? Because buyers are human beings and although there may be trends in certain businesses, (for example advertising is very price-sensitive), what one buyer wants may be different from another.

Consider this; supposing a buyer has always prided himself in getting a good deal and squeezing the supplier on price. But lately he has begun to realise that you get what you pay for, and because he's been experiencing very poor quality, has decided to change his strategy and put quality first. If a salesperson pushes their inexpensive pricing, what chance do you think there is of getting a sale? Similarly, if a buyer has just been let down by their existing supplier, what do you think the main criteria would be in that situation? Delivery of course. So the rule is not to prejudice the buyer with ones own views as to what is important. The secret – which I'm sure you've already discovered – is to ask and find out what a buyer is looking for from a supplier – and talk about that!! A golden rule is that Telling is not Selling – asking is!!

NEEDS IDENTIFICATION

The next stage of the sale involves identifying a buyer's needs and controlling a conversation. Have you ever set yourself a call objective and found that at the end of the call you haven't achieved it or, worse still, found that the dialogue has gone off on a complete tangent, with the buyer obviously taking control? Well, the techniques you can use to avoid this situation are very simple but very effective. If you've been on a sales training course before, I'd be very surprised if you haven't heard about using what's known as open and closed questions.

When you open your mouth and speak, there are really only two things which come out. Either you make a statement or you ask a question. Think about it. Everything you say is either a statement or a question. Well, first of all, the greatest compliment you can give another human being is to ask them a question and listen to their answer. So because buyers are human too, the most logical thing to do is to ask them questions and listen to what they say, as a way of identifying their needs, concerns and buying criteria. When you're telling the buyer about your product or service, you're making statements.

Whilst it's necessary to be able to tell the buyer about what you have on offer, it's best to find out first whether what you're saying is what he or she wants to hear. So, in selling, we ask questions to identify what the buyer's views and needs may be, *before* we start off with all guns blazing about what we want to say. As a buyer once said to me, talk to me about what I want to hear and you'll have more chance of getting a deal! It's so simple really, but so many salespeople don't realise that product knowledge alone does not get you orders.

Of course it's important to know all about your product or service but it's a case of tailoring what you're saying to the needs of the person you're talking to. When I'm selling training, I ask people what they're looking for from a training provider. Some want to know about the trainers' CVs, others want to know about the financial position and stability of the company, and others just want to know what happens in a training room.

I can obviously talk about all those aspects, but I only talk about the things which the individual I'm with at the time wants to hear about. It's logical really isn't it! If you were buying a car in the presence of a salesman and you were interested in how much boot space there was, you might not be so keen to hear all about the engine capacity, and vice versa of course.

The rule is to ask buyers questions about their worries, needs and concerns, their past, present and future difficulties and plans. And about their customers. A buyer who is clear on their buying requirements will appreciate this approach. One who is not so keen or clear will also respond more favourably to being asked genuine questions than being told what you think they should hear. And, finally, you have more chance of a breakthrough by asking questions of the buyer who says they have no interest at all in what you're selling, than you would if you started telling them things.

Think about the last selling situation you were in where afterwards you realised you'd been unable to generate some interest or create a need, and think about what you said . . . and, more importantly, what you asked. And looking back, what questions could you have asked which could've got the buyer more interested. Perhaps you can also think about a call you know is coming up where you think that the interest isn't going to be that strong, and plan some questions you could ask which will show you are interested in seeing how your product or service is going to help them solve a problem.

So, what are open and closed questions? Well a closed question is one which invites a yes or no answer, for example: do you, did I, can we, could I, is it, will there, would you, have I, has it, shall we and should I? You'd ask a closed question when you were closing or testing commitment, for example: 'would you like to go ahead and order or can I go ahead and raise the paperwork?' It can also be used when you want to control the conversation with someone who is highly verbal!

An open question is used to identify information. So if you are probing to discover what a buyer's needs are, or are attempting to understand a buyer's opinion in favour of the competition or against your product, an open question will work better for you than a closed one. An open question would have one of the following words in it – how, what and when, which, why, where and who.

Questions to a buyer might be, how do you see our product assisting with that problem? or when do you think that difficulty would arise the most? You obviously use a combination of open and closed questions every day and don't say, 'Oh, I've just asked a closed question' – we construct language in this way almost unconsciously. But if you want to get into the habit of asking open and closed questions at appropriate times, the behavioural psychologists maintain it takes us three weeks to form or break a habit so long as? motivation and knowledge are present, so it might be a good idea to have the questions written down somewhere that you can easily refer to them for a couple of weeks.

The 'answering a question with a question' technique is very effective for controlling a conversation. A lot of people don't do this because we were all brought up to be polite and we were told 'don't answer a question with a question – it's rude', but in actual fact it's an assertive technique because it takes into account the needs of both parties. So what's the benefit of answering a question with a question? Well, first of all, ask yourself why do people ask us questions. Often it's because they want to know our answer but it can just as often be a way for the person to express the fact that they have an opinion which they want to give us. Think about the last time someone asked you if you'd ever been to Cyprus or what you thought of a new movie at the cinema! It probably meant they had just been or were just going and wanted to tell you all about it!

So when a buyer asks you a question, get into the habit of asking yourself 'is there an opinion behind this question which I need to find out about?' A very good example is if the buyer asks you, 'how much is it?' This question could be another way of saying, 'If the price is within my budget then I will buy'. Another example is if you are asked about delivery or installation dates, it could be another way of the buyer saying, 'If you can supply when I want, then I will order'. In fact those two are examples of questions from a buyer which can also be considered as what's known as a buying signal. So watch out for buying signal questions so that you can respond with a question. If the buyer says 'How much is it?' you can respond with, 'If the price I quote you is within your budget, will you be in a position to order today?' because as a salesperson you are paid to seek commitment, not give information.

A buyer's question can also be a hidden way of expressing a negative opinion and, again, if we answer a question with a question rather than just launching into an answer, it gives us an opportunity to determine where the buyer's negative opinion has come from and puts us in a better position to respond to it. Very often the negative question is prefaced with 'don't you think that . . .?' For example 'don't you think that our requirements are a bit outside of your specification?' To which your logical question would be . . .'in what way?' rather than responding with a statement such as 'well no, because . . .' which would restrict your opportunity to draw out and reassure the person.

A lot of salespeople are in the habit of thinking that they should always answer a buyer's question because it is polite and helpful, and if that is you it will take a while to change the habit. Some people feel more comfortable initially to answer the buyer's question but then to immediately follow it with a question. So, for example, if the buyer says 'how much is it?', you could respond with 'two thousand five hundred pounds inclusive of delivery and service charge . . . how does that fit with your budget?' Or 'two thousand five hundred pounds inclusive of delivery and service charge . . . would delivery on 28th suit you?' However, this still means that you have given a piece of information without attempting to discover what the buyer's views or criteria are, and if the answer you give the buyer doesn't suit them, it may then be that your answer doesn't have as much impact. Let's see why.

If the buyer asks you 'how long has your company been trading?' and you say, 'two years . . . how important is that to you?', then the buyer may answer with, 'well I'm not dealing with an organisation that isn't very experienced in our marketplace'. You then have to work hard to offer the reassurances required. However, if you answered the question with a question straight away, then the outcome could be more positive. So the buyer says, 'how long has your company been trading?' and you say, 'how important is our trading history to you?', then if the buyer says, 'I dealt with a new company once because I thought I'd give them a hand to get on their feet, but they were very inexperienced in our marketplace' then you can respond with, 'well although we have only been trading for two years, we conducted substantial research in your marketplace before we launched our product, and you can rest assured that we also have a wealth of experience in the combined backgrounds of our two directors', and this response is far more likely to eliminate the buyer's fears.

You can then finish off your explanation by asking a commitment-seeking question or continue to control and move the conversation on by asking a probing, open question. Questioning techniques help you to control a call, obtain information, establish two-way communication, demonstrate interest, elicit opinions, isolate feelings, identify doubts and objections, establish feedback and close sales.

A GOOD LISTENER

Being a good questioner is no good unless you're also a good listener. There are four main things taking place in your mind if you are listening effectively:

- The listener thinks ahead of the talker, trying to guess where the oral discourse is leading to, what conclusions will be drawn from the words spoken at the moment;
- The listener weighs the verbal evidence used by the speaker to support the points he or she is making;
- A good listener periodically reviews the portion of the conversation completed so far; and finally
- Throughout the conversation, the listener listens between the lines searching for a meaning which is not necessarily expressed in words, for example convictions, sincerity and emphasis.

A good listener is empathic. In other words they have the ability to see things from another person's point of view, even if they don't agree with it. In selling terms, ego means the desire to have your point of view listened to, and empathy means the desire to ensure that the other person knows that we have understood their viewpoint. A good salesperson can do both. If you are a keen and natural talker, you may be more egotistical than empathic. If you are a keen and natural listener, you will be more empathic than egotistical. It's important to be able to be both. One time in the sales process, for example, when it is important to be empathic is when you are listening to a customer's objection. Talking at them and telling them why your company is wonderful is no good if the customer needs you to listen to their view that the company is bad because of a previous poor experience they've had with you!

SELLING SOLUTIONS

By a series of questions you have proved to the buyer that you are genuinely interested in their needs and problems, and that you are satisfied that you know which aspects of your company and its product or service are relevant to tell the buyer about. When you make statements now, what you say will be tailored to the buyer's needs and what he or she wants to hear.

The next thing to consider is what exactly you are selling. The answer is, solutions. We all sell solutions to problems, irrespective of the product or service we are selling. There are four key things which a buyer wants our product or service to do for them. They want to:

- save,
- solve,

- improve on a situation, and
- gain peace of mind.

What exactly is saved, solved or improved by your product or service? In what way does your supply brings peace of mind? Bear in mind that each individual customer may have other or additional things which they wish to have saved, solved or improved and this is why it is important to identify what is relevant to each individual buyer – by asking them questions. To use sales training jargon, we call it *benefit selling*.

If you pick up your company's product brochure – or indeed any company's product literature – you'll see it will be full of factual information relating to the product; be it technical specification, technical competence, or unique selling points which it can offer over and above the competition. Whilst this is important information, it is very general-ised and that is appropriate for a brochure because it has to attempt to accommodate all the different needs and requirements of any amount of readers. So ask yourself the question 'what can I do that a brochure cannot to improve the chances of getting a sale?' Well the answer is, you can ask questions. A salesperson who relies heavily on a brochure to sell for them, or spends time telling the customer things which can be read in a brochure, is not doing justice to the job of selling. I hope you're more than a talking brochure, because if your company could sell all the products and service it wanted to just by sending out brochures it wouldn't need you! You can ask the customers questions about what they require in a way that a brochure cannot!

Anything about your product or service which is factual we will call a *feature*. What the feature *does* is called an *advantage* and only when the salesperson has identified that the customer has a need for the feature can we consider the advantage to be a benefit. And a benefit is what the feature will *do for the individual* customer you are talking to. People don't buy features, they buy benefits. What your products or services do for them.

An example of this would be if you were selling me coloured white-board markers. A feature of the markers is that they have easily recognisable colour-coded covers on them. The advantage of this is that the user saves time and eliminates mess by not having to remove the covers each time to examine the individual colour of the felt tip under-neath. Now supposing I have an allergy to the material inside felt marker pens and I can only use chalk. I, as the customer, cannot argue with the feature or the advantage of your pens but buying them will not be of benefit to me. So an advantage only becomes a benefit when you have identified that the customer has a need for the feature. In this case, however, if we assume that you have had the opportunity to ask me questions in the first place, you wouldn't be talking to me about these pens but would be showing me how buying your long lasting chalk would be of benefit to me!

Sometimes when I'm talking about this on a training course, salespeople say to me that they are uncomfortable telling the buyer what the benefits are because they are obvious. But that isn't quite the case. Just because you tell someone what something does, doesn't automatically mean that they immediately see how it will save, solve or improve for them. When the salesperson puts it into words for the customer, it highlights the fact that the salesperson is interested in helping the customer. Obvious or not, if a buyer hasn't much to chose between the specification of your product and three or four of your competitors, then it's likely he'll be attracted to the salesperson showing the greatest interest in his individual buying requirements! So to make sure you always tell the customer what's in it for them, try and remember the link phrases, things like 'which means you will get . . .' this enables you to . . . 'therefore you can . . .', and always remember, save, solve, improve and peace of mind.

You can gain the attention and interest of a buyer very effectively by incorporating this at the beginning of a dialogue, on the telephone and even by letter. Having interviewed many buyers and had buyers on courses I can reliably tell you that many salespeople open up a call by saying to the buyer something like, 'I'd like to tell you all about our product . . .', once again using statements rather than questions. How do **you** open up a call?

HANDLING OBJECTIONS

Assuming you have done your preparation, identified or created a need by asking questions and have tailored what you're saying about the product or service to the person you are talking to, you should be well on your way to controlling the call towards a successful outcome. However, even the most prepared and experienced salesperson has to know how to deal with customers' objections.

Research suggests that up to 70 per cent of people in selling don't ask for commitment or close the sale, and two main reasons were given as to why not. First, was fear of rejection. People taking the no's personally. The second was not knowing how to deal with an objection. A lot of salespeople will wait and hope that a buyer will volunteer an order rather than them having to ask for it! So, how do you deal with objections? If you have a method which works already, then of course, don't change it! But if you're having problems dealing with objections, the following tips should help.

Objections normally arise at two distinct times in a sales call. Sometimes they arise before we even get in to see a buyer – from the receptionist or the secretary, then from the buyer right at the beginning before you've even had a chance to ask a question, things like 'I'm not interested', 'I've no time', or 'I'm too busy' and the others come later after you've asked a closing question and they reply with, 'it's too expensive' or 'I'm happy with my current supplier'.

An important thing to realise about objections is that they are actually a buyer's way of saying, 'I am interested but I'm not yet convinced'. An objection is really just a request for more information and it most certainly is not rejection. Rejection is where the person puts the phone down or refuses to converse with you at all. An objection is merely a way of the buyer saying, 'convince me and I'll change my mind', so your attitude to an objection should be positive because it's a chance to start selling.

A lot of salespeople are fearful that they will never be able to answer all the objections they might hear, but in fact, however they might be expressed, objections only come from a few main sources. The decision-maker type objections such as 'I don't have a budget', 'you'll have to speak to someone else' and 'I don't have a need', and the five criteria for buying, price, quality, quantity, delivery or availability and service. Think about it; any objection you hear will be derived from these simple sources. And as I said earlier, if you identify buying criteria in these areas by asking questions, you are unlikely to encounter objections! But if you do, let's look at a simple way of dealing with them.

What do you think is the very first thing you should say when you encounter an objection? Well, before you do anything else it's important to acknowledge the objection because this shows the other person that you respect the fact that they have a point of view. In doing this you're ensuring that they are more likely to listen to your response. So an acknowledgment is something like 'I understand that you think it's a lot of money to pay. . .', or 'I accept you feel it's not important at the current time', or 'I'm delighted you have a supplier at present', and that's all you need to say. Make sure it sounds genuine and that you don't rush it to get it out of the way so that you can head on and say what *you* want to say!

After you have acknowledged the objection, lead naturally into asking a question. Preferably an open question. There are several reasons for asking a question at this point. Firstly, it shows you are interested and concerned with the buyer's viewpoint. Secondly, it shows that you are attempting to fully understand the buyer's opinion, and, thirdly, it can create an opportunity for you to have the buyer justify their viewpoint rather than you having to defend the objection. Let me give you some examples.

If a buyer says to you, 'That's too expensive', the question which follows the acknowledgment could be, 'What are you comparing it to?'. Similarly, if a buyer says, 'I'm happy with my current supplier', you could ask, 'In what ways do you think they could improve their service to you?' And if a buyer says, 'we don't consider that important', or 'I'm not interested', your question could be, 'how are you protecting the equipment at the moment then?'. If the buyer says they have no budget, you could ask the question, 'When will you be looking to invest?'

Assuming you get an answer to your question, and that the buyer elaborates on their concern, you have now got to say something so that they change their mind in your favour. What approach do you take here? . . . well think about it. The buyer has really said, 'this is my concern. If you can deal with it then we could be in business', so what do you use to overcome the objection, or provide what's necessary for them to change their mind? Well, quite simply, you must give them a positive reason to do so; in other words show them a benefit, or you must show them where they would have a problem or be missing out on a solution if they didn't change their mind.

Don't forget, people buy because they have a need to save, solve or improve or to gain peace of mind. Remember that a benefit is something which is tailored and relevant to the needs of the individual buyer or buyers you're talking to. You only know what the benefits might be when you've asked questions and identified and established a need and had this acknowledged by the buyer. Before you launch into reminding the buyer of the benefits of going ahead and attempting to eliminate the objection, it's important for you to attempt to gain some, what is known as, 'advanced commitment' from the buyer.

What advanced commitment really means is that you're saying, 'if I am successful in dealing with that point to your satisfaction, then will you change your mind in my favour and go ahead and do business with me?'. This is a perfectly businesslike thing for you to do and you should regard yourself as having a professional right to attempt to gain this advanced commitment because you are paid to seek commitment, not just to give information. What you are saying to the client is, 'I am perfectly happy to spend as long as is necessary discussing your concerns, however all I'm asking in advance is to know that if I'm successful at putting your mind at rest, are we going to do business?' Selling is presenting in a manner people find acceptable, and a professional buyer will respect you for using this approach. So if the buyer says, 'It's too expensive', your advanced commitment question would be, 'If I can prove to you that the money we're asking you to pay is justified in the service and quality we're providing, will you go ahead and order?' and if they say, 'I'm happy with my current supplier' then you could respond with, 'If I can reassure you that we can offer you the same if not better levels of service as your existing supplier, will you consider giving us a trial order?' Or, if the buyer says, 'I won't order from you because you let me down in the past', you could say, 'If I can show you that things have substantially improved since you had that unfortunate experience, would you reconsider dealing with us?'

There are only two logical answers to this closed question. The buyer is going to say yes, no (or maybe, which is treated as a no). If he says yes, then you continue on with your benefits and justification, knowing you have his advanced commitment. If he says no, it means he probably has some other concerns as well in which case you can say, 'that suggests something else is concerning you, tell me, what is it?' and when he tells you, you return to the advanced commitment technique.

So for example, if he first objects on price and secondly that you can't offer an overnight delivery, you can say, 'If I can reassure you that our fees are most competitive within the industry *and* that you'd be missing out on the additional benefits of dealing with us if you chose not to buy because of our delivery schedule, then would you reconsider placing an order?', and if he says maybe, you could say, 'your hesitation suggests there is something else which you're not sure about, tell me what is it?'

Now let me give you some examples of how you provide the proof or reassurance or justification you've promised the buyer. If you get the objection well into a call after you've had a chance to establish some form of need and discuss the benefits of your solution, it is easy to say something like, 'whilst I appreciate that establishing the additional budget is not something you're keen to do, I'm sure you'd agree that the overall benefits you'll gain from buying now, more than justify the increased investment required and will in fact improve the downtime which you told me earlier is costing you money at the moment'. If you get the objection at the beginning of the call when you've had little or no time to ask questions or establish any kind of need, then you can respond with, 'In order for me to prove it to your satisfaction, I need to ask you a few questions, is that all right with you?', and by using this question you have either created an opportunity to develop a need at best or, at worst, you have not apologised for your product or wasted time talking about something that the buyer doesn't want to hear.

It is a simple procedure:

- acknowledge,
- question,
- advanced commitment, then
- provide proof.

And of course, remember the golden rule – once you have successfully overcome an objection, close. In other words, say something like, 'on the basis that I've now clarified your concern, do you have an order number for me?'

If the objection comes from the secretary or receptionist, for example 'he's not interested', or 'you'll have to tell me what it's about', then you again have the choice of a question or a statement. I'm sure you know that a question is the only way to deal with the situation. You could say, 'what I required in the first instance was some information. Could you tell me please, what is Mr Smith currently doing to preserve the x, y and z in view of changing legislation in a, b and c?' Don't forget, the receptionist is only doing their job and it is of course quite helpful to you if you can make an ally of them. Sometimes the best you can hope for is to get some form of commitment from the secretary. For example, if you're told that the buyer is in a meeting and you ask what time they'll be free, you can then say 'so if I call back at 4.15 will there be any reason why you can't put me through?'

Very often buyers will ask us questions which should really be treated as objections. The classic example is when we're asked for a discount. Quite often, I'm afraid, salespeople will just agree the discount and sometimes they will attempt to get an increased order in return for the discount. This happens of course because the salesperson is frightened they will lose the order if they don't agree the discount. This is why it's important for you to understand the margins involved in supplying your product, but really your aim is to sell your product or service at maximum profit margins.

Perhaps the best way I can help you here is to ask you to check out your own attitude. If you think about it, the buyer asking for a discount over and above the going rate is no different to you asking the buyer if they will pay more if they are satisfied with the product! You could even say this to a buyer with a smile in your voice! If someone asks you for a discount, you could respond with the question, 'what would you like me to take away from the product so that I can decrease the price?', and of course it's unlikely that they will ask you to decrease specification or decrease their credit terms or push out delivery schedules. What the question does is show them that they get what they pay for.

Another objection we sometimes hear which is not very specific is something like 'I'll think about it', so how do you respond to that? Many sales people will say, 'when can I get back to you?' but unfortunately when buyers say, 'I'll think about it', it doesn't mean they're going to ask their secretaries to hold all calls whilst they think about your proposals! What it normally means is that they have a specific objection which they're uncomfortable to mention and we have to make it easy for them to do so. And the best way of doing that is to ask an open question, something like 'tell me, what exactly is it that's causing you concern. Some salespeople will use a fear-inducing technique here and say something like, 'well I appreciate you're going to think about it but may I just suggest you don't take too long as our special offer will be finished next week'. You can use this technique too if it is appropriate for the buyer you're talking to.

Don't forget, selling is presenting in a manner people find acceptable and it's all about what the buyer is comfortable with, not what fits with your comfort zones. Don't let your own fear or discomfort prevent you from using a technique which will work for you. In fact we sometimes invite objections because of our own attitude to them. The typical situation which I come across is the salesperson who thinks or feels that their product is priced too high. Because of this, when they are speaking with the customer the salesperson doesn't sell very effectively and doesn't get the order and consequently feels that the price is even more difficult to sell – and because of this sells even less effectively with the next customer and in fact creates a vicious circle which often ends with the salesperson apologising for the price!

'CLOSING'

Closing techniques are the logical conclusion to everything else you've been doing so far. It is part of a salesperson's job to seek commitment, but unfortunately a lot of people in selling wait for the customer to volunteer an order – which doesn't happen as often as we'd like of course! One of the reasons why is because people aren't often comfortable making decisions. How familiar is this situation? You say to someone, 'would you like to go to dinner?', and they say, 'yes where will we go?', and you say, 'I don't know, where would you like to go?,' and when you eventually get there you say, 'what are you having to eat?', and they say, 'I don't know, what are you having?', and so it goes on! None of us enjoy making decisions and a buyer is no different. So by *asking* the buyer we are encouraging and supporting them towards a decision, rather than leaving them alone with their discomfort.

There are lots of books and training courses which cover all the different closing techniques and give them their relevant titles; however I believe the most important rule of closing is to *ask*. In other words, don't let a fear of rejection stop you from asking. After all, most buyers expect to be asked for the order and it is only your own dedication, discipline and determination which will make sure the buyers expectation is met.

Another important point about closing is the misconception that there is some magical time when we should close the sale. There isn't. You don't have to wait until the end of a call to close. Think about it logically, you are constantly looking for opportunities to close. For example, as we discussed earlier, you close when you have successfully overcome an objection. You close when there is nothing else to be said or done, you close when you can't think of anything else to say, and you close when you hear what's known as a buying signal.

A buying signal is never as obvious as someone volunteering an order I'm afraid! When the buyer says something like, 'I've heard good things about your company' or 'that sounds interesting' or 'that might help us', we are hearing a buying signal. The problem is sometimes we are so preoccupied with what we want to say next that we don't hear them! So a good salesperson is also a good detective and is constantly listening out for buying signals and clues that the buyer may be ready to make a decision.

The reason there are lots of different closing techniques is because some techniques work better with some people than others. The important thing is to try and master all the techniques so that you're comfortable with them, and don't fall into the trap of only using one or two that you're used to. One buying signal is called the direct question close, where you ask a simple, closed question, for example, 'would you like to go ahead?' or 'can you give me an order number today?' or 'will you give me the order?' Another tried and tested technique is called the assumed close where you are less direct in your question, for example, 'where would you like us to send the invoice?' or 'which day would be most convenient for delivery?' And then we have the alternative close whereby you give the person a positive choice of two things but either answer would suit you, for example, 'would you like our staff to install during working hours or after your staff have left', or if you're looking for an appointment 'would Tuesday at 2.35 or Wednesday at 3.40 be more convenient for you?'

Another technique is known as the 'If . . . then' close, whereby you would say, 'If I can guarantee to have it delivered by Wednesday week, then would you be able to give me a purchase order number today?' The final rule of closing is that once you have a commitment – then shut up! Don't do what a lot of untrained salespeople do and that is to talk yourself out of an order. Also don't forget, if you are unsuccessful – and no one is successful all of the time – and someone has said no to you, it is a good time to ask for a lead or a referral. Psychologically, the buyer may be feeling a bit guilty or even sorry for you because they've had to say no, so they could very well feel relieved to have the chance to give you something.

ATTITUDE

Your attitude to selling is also important. If you tell yourself too often that you're not going to get an order or hit your target, then that's what's likely to happen! But the reverse can apply, you can attract the outcomes you want by thinking about them – it's called the power of visualisation. We've all heard stories about the power of the human mind, the mother who gets superhuman strength to lift the car which her daughter is trapped under for example, and the fact that we only use about five per cent of our brain's power, so whilst it sounds like a cliché, it's actually very true – if you think you can, you can!

There are hundreds of books on PMA, getting a positive mental attitude, but the techniques you use are less important than the fact that you do something to keep yourself in a positive frame of mind. Of course there's nothing better than a big order for giving you a buzz, but perhaps I can give you a tip to help you keep focused. It's a tip which actors use to convey certain emotions in a film. If you aren't feeling particularly positive, find yourself some private space somewhere and close your eyes. Think about an incident in your life when you felt particularly confident or positive. Allow your mind to play out the whole scene or incident and don't rush it. Enjoy every moment! What you should find is that the feelings you experienced during this event also return to you.

Life is a balance, and whether we like it or not our private life does affect our work and our work does affect our private life. Just remember that when you're not at work, it's worth being careful about the kind of company you keep. If you have too many people around you who are telling you about their problems, their lack of opportunities or their failures, it will work as a drain on your positive attitude. And I'm sure you've heard the expression that unless you're right with yourself, you can't be of any help to others, whoever they may be!

NEGOTIATION

Selling and negotiation are closely linked but what is the difference between them? The best way to answer this is to say that in selling the desire to sell is greater than the desire to buy, whereas with negotiating the desire to buy is as strong as the desire to sell; it is merely the terms and conditions of doing business which require finalising. So it would logically follow that most negotiations occur with existing customers and people whom we've done business with for some time. And the terms and conditions centre around the five criteria for buying.

The key difference between negotiating and selling, I believe, is in the salesperson's attitude. In selling, because we seem to want the business more than the buyer seems to want to give it to us, the attitude that many salespeople develop is one of fear and gratitude towards the buyer. I often work with teams of salespeople who do business with multinational companies or organisations which have near monopolies in their market-place. These salespeople have the belief that it's the buyer who calls the shots. They've convinced themselves of this to the point where they don't bother trying to get a better deal.

Consider the fact that in any realistic negotiation both parties are trying to get the best deal possible but that neither party ends up with everything that they want. What you should be trying to achieve is what we call a win–win situation, where both *think* that they've got the best deal. If one party squeezes the other too much then the outcome would be termed a win–lose situation, and of course sometimes, through the opening stance being too exaggerated or greedy or some other breakdown factor, no deal is struck and this is called a lose–lose. So think about the psychology that goes on in negotiations. Both parties do want to reach an outcome, but if one party admits this too readily or openly to the other, then the second party has the upper hand. In other words, if the salesperson appears too keen or too grateful, the buyer is going to aim for and usually gets a better price or a better overall deal. That's why it is so important for a salesperson to know when an order is not profitable to him, and when it is better for him to walk away from the deal.

It's also very important that, without being aggressive, the salesperson has a confident, proud and healthy attitude towards their own and the buyer's position in the negotiation. One of the things that helps you to have the right attitude is to make sure you have done your homework before a call so that you can be planned and prepared.

Another important aspect of negotiation is 'trading concessions'. It is what two people do when they are attempting to reach an outcome somewhere in the middle of what they both want. In selling we tend to give away concessions, whereas in negotiation we trade them. For example, in a selling situation, if a buyer were to ask you to include special loading facilities or technical training at no extra cost, you may be tempted or likely to agree this for fear of losing the order.

In negotiations, because you are constantly reminding yourself that the other side wants to do business with you just as much as you do with them, it is not dangerous to attempt to get something in return for the concession. So you might say, 'in order for us to supply the loading equipment whenever you require it, we will have to view it as a dedicated resource. In order for us to cover the cost of this it will be necessary for us to include a small charge for raising the customised documentation', or you might say, 'if I agree to supply the specialised loading equipment at no extra charge, then will you agree to specify in advance the exact times you will require the equipment?'. You may recognise here the if . . . then technique which we used earlier for dealing with objections. It is very effective in negotiations for trading concessions.

What exactly is a concession? Well it is something we give away. In selling we truly do give away our benefits, but in a negotiation we trade our benefits so that when we give one, we try and get something in return. There is a golden rule here. You give away that which is important to the buyer but is cheap for you to give. You make what is cheap for you to give look expensive.

Let's say for example that supplying specialist technical training is not difficult or expensive for you to give, but that you know it is something the buyer wants or needs. In a selling situation you might say, 'yes, that's no problem' if you were asked for it. But in a negotiation, you would make it look hard and look for something in return. For example, you might say, 'supplying specialist technical training is not something we would normally offer, but if I were able to provide you with the training every Monday could you in return guarantee that you will not introduce penalty clauses in the event of an unlikely late delivery on our part?'.

As you can see, the language and vocabulary you use is very important, but equally so is your attitude towards using the technique. You have a professional right to pursue a deal which is fair to the buyer but is profitable to your company. And don't forget that buyers are taught exactly the same techniques on courses! In fact in a true negotiation, there is no buyer or seller, it is merely two people trying to get the best deal for their companies. If you are satisfied that you do offer high quality and service at a fair price, then a buyer will respect you for standing up for this.

Another thing to be careful of is how you treat objections in a negotiation. In selling, we learn and tend to deal with objections as they arise, and as you learned earlier we overcome them with benefits. In a negotiation, what sounds like an objection is usually just the buyer's way of trying to get more out of you, so instead of tackling the objection head on straight away, try and develop the habit of treating it as if the buyer was just giving you something from his or her shopping list. A good way of responding to an objection then is to say 'well that's something which we may be able to consider when we have examined all the aspects of this order, and I'm prepared to make a note of it', and then regain control of the situation by asking a question.

The high-achieving salespeople I mentioned earlier had a special ability to negotiate within their own organisations first before they even started negotiating with external customers. Is this something you find you have to do? Sometimes we have to encourage other departments or even our own sales management to agree to do something outside our own normal systems and procedures so that we have the flexibility to trade concessions. The term for this is *constants* and *variables*. A good negotiator is always looking for constants which can be changed into variables so as to increase the possible concessions list. For example, if you don't normally send out weekly statements – the norm being monthly – if it is important to the customer and you can get something worthwhile in return for agreeing this, it's worth negotiating within your own company to get this agreed. You've just turned a constant into a variable!

A lot of people ask me, 'When do I know whether I'm in a selling situation or a negotiation?' and that is not obvious or easy to answer. A selling situation normally occurs when the salesperson has made the approach to the customer and has had to do or say something to increase the buyer's desire to purchase. If the buyer has contacted you, then I would definitely recommend that you treat the possibility as a negotiation. Once the buyer has the need and is interested to buy, it is merely the terms and conditions which he or she will be looking to get the best of, from you and from your competition.

Annex A
Stress Management – Depression

B. L. Corfield, MRPS

INTRODUCTION

Stress and its effects on people in all walks of life from the shopfloor worker to the senior executive is becoming more widely recognised and less of a taboo subject. All of us are subject to stress in one way or another, and in some circumstances prolonged stress can lead to depressive illness. This paper attempts to provide some simple guidelines for managers who may one day find themselves dealing with a member of staff who is suffering from depression.

This paper is not about the clinical management of depression which must be left to the professionals. It is a manager's view about what can be done by managers to help an individual through a very difficult period and speed recovery to a full and productive life again.

WHAT IS DEPRESSION

We have all heard the terms, 'nervous breakdown' and 'executive burnout' amongst others. They are euphemisms for depressive illness and anxiety states and other emotional disorders which can result from stress. I shall concentrate on depression. I choose the term illness, because depression is organic disease, readily characterised, diagnosable and treatable with anti-depressants. There is a little less than a 1:5 chance of an individual suffering from depression sometime during their life, so it is not an uncommon affliction.

At the risk of being a little technical there are two types of depression, one that seems to affect certain individuals for which there is no apparent cause; it is called endogenous depression. The other, possibly more widespread, is as a result of the individual's reaction to external events and stimuli and is called reactive depression. Both are characterised by a lowering of the mood state as neuro-transmitter levels in the brain are depleted (a simple but not entirely accurate description). Anti-depressants work by restoring the normal physiological neuro-transmitter levels and actions.

199

The causes of depression are varied and idiosyncratic and depend on such things as circumstances, personality, family history, coping behaviours, level and duration of stress.

Typically, as the duration and/or level of stress increases, the person becomes exhausted by the effort of managing the situation. Maladaptive behavioural responses to the situation occur by which the person tries to protect themself from the pressures that they are facing. This in turn leads to various physiobiological and mental changes taking place until the person has the recognisable signs and symptoms of depression.

What does depression feel like to the patient? John Bunyan in *Pilgrims Progress* writing in the 17th century, described depression as the 'Slough of Despond'. I cannot think of a better description. The depressed person feels awful. Anxiety often accompanies depression and gnaws away at the person's vitality during waking hours and the outlook is bleak and hopeless. Sleeplessness is another characteristic feature which further saps energy leading to extreme tiredness. It is truly a living hell. Living or working with a depressed person can be very difficult and emotionally draining for family and friends and requires patience and a lot of understanding.

HOW TO RECOGNISE DEPRESSION

How would a manager recognise depression in a member of staff? Unlike a broken arm or leg it is not very visible; the Band Aid is stuck on the brain and covered by skull and scalp. For some individuals depression is a possible outcome of psychological trauma, or major adverse life events, so there may be a history of somebody who has been under severe stress for a prolonged period of time, or a catastrophic event has occurred such as the death of a child for instance. The most obvious signs to a manager and colleagues are loss of performance, mood changes, increased absenteeism, loss of concentration, the inability to make decisions or plan ahead, a dejected and tired appearance, withdrawal from group interactions, an apparent loss of personal confidence. On enquiry, the person may attempt to put on a brave face, or conversely break down. There is a lot of guilt, fear and embarrassment associated with depression and the person may not be very forthcoming to their manager. If the manager is concerned that all is not well, then the Medical Officer should be approached for further assessment and referral. Clinical depression can present in different degrees of severity and the correct treatment and supportive therapy is essential.

WHAT CAN MANAGERS DO?

Firstly, to recognise that this person is ill and not 'swinging the lead'. Secondly, patience is needed because recovery can be a long process. After the start of medication there may be a delay of about two weeks before the mood begins to lift and the person starts to feel any better. Full recovery may take many months and is concerned with the person confronting the problems that they are faced with, finding solutions, learning new coping behaviours and most importantly, rebuilding their shattered self-esteem. This last process may take a year or two in some cases. It is also an area in which the manager can be most helpful.

Depending on the severity of the depression, the person may be be advised to take sick leave to reduce the pressure whilst drug therapy and other supportive measures are commenced, or continue at work. On return to work or if they do not take sick leave, they will probably be functioning at a much reduced level to normal.

It is most important that everything is done to preserve, protect and bolster the person's self-esteem. This cannot be over-emphasized. This means a sympathetic approach is required on the part of the manager. A 'buck your ideas up' pep talk is at best unhelpful and should be avoided. It is a natural reaction to loss of performance and is understandable but in this instance counter-productive.

The scope of the person's work, targets and deliverables should be reviewed and an action plan of limited duration and achievement consistent with the person's coping ability should be agreed. Small, achievable successes do so much to convince the person that they are not an abject failure. Positive feedback is very important in recognising what may be a modest achievement that would normally go unrecognised. Criticism, even if meant to be constructive, can add to the burden of the depressed person and can assume proportions quite outside the reality of the comment. The last thing a depressed person needs to be told is that he or she is useless and not up to scratch; he knows he is not performing as usual and tells himself that several hundred times a day

The most effective long-term cure is to work with the person to help him learn about himself, understand what has led him into depressive illness, learn to cope better with stressful situations because they cannot be avoided entirely and to help rebuild a positive view of himself. Professional counselling may be required and this can be reinforced by an understanding manager.

Regular meetings are desirable to build confidence, talk about problems and feelings. Articulating a problem often leads to finding a solution that the person will own and do something about. Finding a mentor may also be desirable, recognising the fear/unwillingness of talking to one's manager about some issues.

The person will usually start to feel better as the drug therapy starts working and will find that his energy levels increase as normal sleep patterns return. The loss of memory, indecisiveness and lack of concentration can be quite perplexing and frightening to a normally capable individual. It can result in a loss of confidence of varying degrees of severity. Reassurance is needed that this is only temporary and that it will return as the illness regresses. Again, the manager can do so much to help in this area

The manager will find that managing a depressed person is consumptive of his time and at times very frustrating. It seems inexplicable that a normally competent member of staff just appears to have gone completely 'off the boil' and exhibits this strange behaviour. Within reason, however, the manager will wish to do his best for the welfare of his staff. He may himself gain some insight into the nature of work and stress management that will better equip him for the future.

CONCLUSION

Clearly, these simple actions can help speed the road to recovery and enable the person to once more lead a useful and productive life. Psychological trauma does have its positive side. Most people emerge from it scarred, but definitely the wiser, more resilient and better able to cope with the vicissitudes of life. Work is a main source of self-esteem and self-worth to most individuals and when illness does strike, a knowledgeable manager can do much to aid the recovery process.

Stress is with us and all around us and in my view we can do much to help ourselves and others cope especially through the rougher patches of life and learn from our experience.

I hope that this paper will have given you some insight into depression, what can be done to help and what is best avoided. It is an illness, the person suffering from depression isn't morally suspect or lazy and it is worth remembering that depression is no respecter of rank or wealth.

Annex B
Standards and
Regulations

THE ISO 9000 STANDARD

ISO 9000 comprises of an internationally recognised set of standards for use by suppliers and purchasers, explaining the requirements of a quality-oriented system. They are practical standards which identify the basic disciplines and specify the procedures and criteria to ensure that products or services meet the customer's requirements. What is more, they are relevant and practical to companies of all sizes in all industries, not just to a few large firms.

What are the benefits of ISO 9000 accreditation?

The benefits of applying ISO 9000 standards to your business procedures are real. Quality systems will reduce waste and time-consuming re-working of designs and processes by 'getting it right the first time'. This will increase your profits both directly and also by allowing you to compete for increased share in a highly competitive marketplace.

Which of the ISO 9000 standards should my company apply for?

ISO 9000 is divided into three distinct parts; you can therefore choose which is best suited to your operation and your customers' requirements.

- ISO 9001 specification for design/development, manufacture, installation and servicing.
- ISO 9002 specification for manufacture and installation.
- ISO 9003 specification for final inspection and test.

Both manufacturing and service companies can apply for any of these standards.

One of my competitors has BS 5750 accreditation. What is the difference?

There is no difference. ISO 9001/9002/9003 are exactly equivalent to BS 5750 Parts 1/2/3 and also to European standard EN 2001, 29002 and 29003.

How long will it take to achieve certification?

This will depend on the size of your company and the complexity of its operations. It will also depend on the degree to which your existing systems 'conform' to ISO 9000 standards, as this will be a key factor in determining the amount of work required to implement a documented quality system.

Once we have achieved certification, how do we keep it?

Commitment to quality principles by top management is essential from the time a company first undertakes to go for ISO 9000. It is a continuation of this level of commitment which will maintain your ISO certification.

Can we lose our certification once we have achieved it?

Yes. All approved companies are periodically re-assessed to ensure that the quality management system is being adhered to. Certification can be withdrawn if this is not found.

Our products and systems are already first class – we don't need a certificate!

You may know this to be the case, and perhaps your existing customers may agree with your claim, but the potential first-time customer does not have such knowledge. If the potential customer has a choice between your company and a competitor who boasts certification to ISO 9000, then he's going to choose the quality-oriented competitor every time. Remember, if your company is so good then ISO 9000 could be implemented very quickly and easily.

What is it going to cost?

The cost of the programme is heavily based on the size of the company and how much the current level of systems complies with the ISO standard.

What is the difference between ISO for a manufacturing company and a service company?

There is very little difference between the two. A manufacturing company would be required to monitor the quality of the product throughout the production process. A service company is required to monitor the quality of its service so that the quality complies to the customer's wishes. This monitoring would take place in key areas that directly affect the quality of the service given. For example: the taking of a customer's order. Do you understand exactly what the customer is asking for?

Will we need more people to establish and maintain the standard?

This is dependent on the current system that your company has in place. Normally companies will be required to do some initial work to establish a system that conforms to the standard. After that a person is assigned the task of Quality Controller which depending on the size of the company is normally not a full-time position.

* * *

WHITE PAPER PRESENTATION FOR DMA TELEPHONE MARKETING

Conference attendees, June 1996, Almskog and Frydman Communications

This White Paper presentation may be of interest to readers involved in the technical aspects of call centre development.

Introduction

The evolution of call center technology can best be understood in terms of traditional role and corporate outlook. Despite the success of early applications, such as service agencies, catalogs, and high-end customer service, call centers were typically compared to other labor intensive, routine back-office functions. Niche markets, unique requirements, and limited integration options meant proprietary technology solutions.

The 1990s have seen consideration of service quality and delivery costs force fundamental changes in priorities. Call centers are increasingly viewed as strategic assets, with critical systems needs.

Call center technology projects are larger and more complicated. While the selection and management of various call center systems was often treated as a departmental function, integration and shared application resources have created a new level of technology overhead. Significant technology initiatives are now reaching smaller centers, even into the 50 to 75 station range, which just several years ago saw very limited integration investments. This trend is particularly true for European start-ups, which are most likely smaller than their U.S. counterparts, but have proven more than willing to invest in technology.

How will the call center of the future change? While the list of most popular GUI (Graphical User Interface) development environments seems to change quite frequently, users are more interested in applications and solutions.

This analysis is intended to provide a look at the most critical areas of call center technology, with a focus on what to expect and how best to manage it.

Critical Technologies

This section covers five basic categories of call center technology:

- ACD
- IVR
- Contact Management
- CTI
- Long Distance Networks

Automatic Call Distributors

The primary differences between ACD products involve conditional call routing options, integrated voice processing, reporting, and capacity. This market will continue to be bitterly competitive, but with vendor strategy focused on packaging and frequent upgrades rather than price reductions.

With system prices staying in the $1500 to $4000 per station range, combined with new release upgrade costs reaching $100 00 +, depending on product and configuration, ACD will continue to be a priority for PBX vendors, such as Lucent Technologies (previously AT & T) Nortel and Siemens Rolm.

Some predictions to watch for:

- Call overflow features for networked ACDs will improve. Currently, most products are limited to one-to-one relationships for overflow to alternate sites (namely site A can look at site B, but not at B and C simultaneously.
- Bundled solutions will include workforce management, to provide robust forecasting and agent scheduling. The first example of this kind is Nortel's MaxCaster for Meridian Max, which is based on the TCS TeleCenter-system. Likewise, ACD routing options will include variations of today's high-end solutions for call-by-call routing, such as Geotel and IEX. However, such

products will not reach the under 600 + station networks without significant price reductions, vs. current $100 000 to $200 000 per site entry cost.

- Multimedia ACD capabilities will bring video queuing. Early trials of video kiosk calling (such as financial services) showed promise, but proved highly inefficient, as video stations required dedicated agents. Intecom, Lucent, and Rockwell indicate plans to have video queuing solutions available by late 1997. Multimedia ACD should be considered in terms of integrated call handling; with video clips or Internet access options replacing audio delay messages.

- Despite the continued growth of generic call processing components and software drivers, as well as CTI modules bundled with standard network operating system packages, ACD will not become another LAN application. The notion of 'ACD in a PC server' will be limited to low-end, casual applications. ACD access to LAN resources, such as database servers, is available today, however, any replacement of proprietary platforms implies considerable advances in LAN server stability and traffic control.

Interactive Voice Response

IVR often provides the most significant productivity gains relative to other call center technologies. It is not uncommon to find users with 70 per cent to 80 per cent of calls handled without agent intervention. In fact, some vertical markets, such as consumer financial services and airlines, have made IVR a competitive necessity.

Some predictions to watch for:

- Speech recognition will mature quickly. Depending on applications, current digit recognizers, such as VCS and VPC, can yield accuracy rates as high as 95 per cent for continuously spoken account numbers. The distinction between continuous and discrete recognition should not be underestimated, as the latter requires 'artificial' prompts for each digit.

- The next steps in speech recognition are word spotting and natural language understanding. Vendors such as BBN Hark and Nuance offer extensive vocabulary engines which effectively eliminate the need for cumbersome sampling to introduce new words. Natural language understanding uses digit recognition and word spotting inputs to infer context. Although production installations are limited, IVR vendors will continue their efforts to build interfaces for word spotting. Successful applications, such as directory assistance, will drive user demand. For most platforms, the most significant new feature requirement will be 'talk over', to allow the caller to interrupt and be recognized, much like 'key ahead' in today's touch tone applications. Natural language understanding requires considerable product integration and likely remains several years away from routine availability.

- Internet access to IVR applications will become routine. This will reduce integration effort by linking web browsers to established IVR applications and facilitate screen sharing, namely an agent helping a caller through web based transaction. Vendors such as Edify, Lucent Technologies and Pheriphonics have recently released Internet Access modules.

- IVR will grow beyond the call center by adding workflow features. Transaction processing typically requires tight links between IVR and legacy systems. This makes an IVR platform ideally suited for downstream management tasks, such as routing or exception handling.

Contact Management

Contact management applications can be defined as providing call guides or scripts, event reporting, database functions, strategy for outbound calling, interfaces to other applications, and telephony links.

This part of the call center technology marketplace has experienced the greatest turmoil. While an ACD or IVR can be viewed as a turnkey system with limited architecture impact, contact management is most effective where access to enterprise-wide data is readily available. This means both technical support and end-user flexibility.

Some predictions to watch for:

- The lack of clear market leaders and a wide choice of robust GUI development tools will prompt a growing trend towards in-house or custom development, rather than turnkey solutions.
- Proprietary predictive dialing platforms will disappear in favor of CTI-based solutions. ACD vendors will gradually improve their call progress detection capabilities, and dialer vendors are motivated by the higher margins of software vs. customized hardware sales.
- The shift to CTI-based predictive dialing will mean more efficient call blending solutions, with no need for connections between two switches or alternating call control. However, the actual value of call blending will vary by application. For example, inbound and outbound collections, or inbound service and outbound follow-up are often effectively combined, while inbound service and outbound cold calling are not.
- Much like IVR, web technology will impact contact management needs. As an alternative to IVR, access to a web-browser can be provided by a CTI gateway. Corporate data, such as product information or pricing updates, will move to intranet access, in order to allow for common user interfaces with reduced security risks.
- Rapid change has also brought a new world of technical support issues. Developers with contact management experience are particularly scarce, and most integration firms are small, with many integration projects falling into the often dangerous 'one off' category. Along with purely technical requirements, skills needed for user system administrators can be equally challenging.

Computer Telephone Integration

While users and providers of contact management applications have been forced to deal with rapid change, CTI continues to be misunderstood.

Applications can range from simple screen-pops based on DNIS, or Dialed Number Identification Service, to complex voice-data transfers between sites or host control of ACD functions.

The emergence of Microsoft's TAPI and Novell's TSAPI CTI gateways hold the promise of lower costs and easier implementation. As compared to CallPath and a variety of native (specific to each ACD interface) CTI products, software costs are considerably lower, but stability problems and feature gaps have left most high-end users skeptical.

Some predictions to watch for:

- Microsoft and Novell products will mature and compete effectively with CallPath and native solutions. However, CTI gateway pricing is a poor indicator of implementation costs. Integration efforts will continue to be complicated by individual ACD features and the lack of close cooperation between ACD and CTI gateway vendors.
- With no substantial reduction in overall costs for more complex CTI applications, economic considerations will remain troublesome, and spending may be justified in terms of service quality benefits, not incremental efficiency gains. For example, IVR and CTI are often considered as a combined initiative, but long term gains are rarely comparable.
- In addition to screen sharing, CTI products will support Internet and intranet voice messaging and live web calling.

Long Distance Networks

Call center users have traditionally taken a somewhat cynical approach to how long-distance works. Products were essentially generic, network technology difficult to understand, and other carriers followed AT&T's lead when it came to tariffs.

Faced with shrinking margins and the promise of bitter competition in the form of RBOC (Regional Bell Operating Company) entries, the 'big three' (AT&T, MCI and Sprint) have worked hard to find alternatives.

Some predictions to watch for:

- Carriers see tremendous potential in value-added services, such as network queuing, network IVR, and transaction processing. With ordinary usage rates for large, competitive contracts now falling as low as $.065 per minute for dedicated inbound and outbound, value-added service can mean effective premiums of 400 per cent and more.
- Network ACD and IVR will continue to be niche products with limited flexibility, high usage rates and few, if any, CTI options.
- Voice over Internet solutions are currently speculative at best, with compression rates poorly suited for voice communications, but the lure of 'free' calling will see a continuing spiral of disputes between long distance carriers, Internet access providers, and software developers.

*   *   *

REGULATIONS AND REGULATORY BODIES

To prevent unsolicited outbound calls to consumers:

The Telephone Preference Service
1-202-955-5030

FTC trade regulation rules:

Public Reference Branch
Room 130
Federal Trade Commission
Washington, D.C. 20580
1-202-326-2222
www.ftc.gov

Information-Handling Guidelines:

Privacy Rights Clearinghouse
1717 Kettner Ave., Suite 105
San Diego, CA 92101
1-619-298-3396
www.privacyrights.org

For ethical guidelines and information on privacy laws and regulations:

Direct Marketing Association
1120 Avenue of the Americas
New York, NY 10036
1-212-768-7277
www.the-dma.org

Telephone Research Ethics:

American Association for Public Opinion Research
P.O. Box 1248
Ann Arbor, MI 48106
1-313-764-3341
www.aapor.org

Annex C
Example Forms

CUSTOMER SATISFACTION SURVEY

The typical contents one would expect to find in a report outlining a survey of customer satisfaction:

- Executive Summary
- Summary of Results
- Objectives of Research
- Research Methodology.

  - survey method
  - survey response
  - sample design
  - sample selection
  - sample reliability

- Profile of Respondents:

  - main suppliers
  - demand for product

- How Suppliers are Chosen:

  - commencement of supply
  - characteristics of a 'good' supplier

- Satisfaction with level of Service:

  - your company compared to other suppliers
  - who is most dissatisfied with your company

- Scope for Improvement:

  - what your customers complain about
  - why respondents do not consider your company

- Why Buy from Your Company:

  - why respondents would consider being supplied by you
  - why buy from you rather than other suppliers

- Tables

- Appendices:
  - the questionnaire
  - lists used

PRIMARY (P) AND SECONDARY (S) CALL OBJECTIVES

1. Prospect Call	P.	To secure commitment to visit
	S.	To advertise company/send brochure or literature
2. Cold Call (new prospect)	P.	Promote name and existence of our company
	S.	Send further information
3. Customer Liaison Call	P.	Expel fears and sort out problems
	S.	Build back dented image
4. Cash Collection Call	P.	Secure promise/commitment to pay
	S.	Keep image intact and go on selling
5. Appointment-making Call	P.	Make definite but realistic appointment
	S.	Mention all range of services
6. Repeat Ordering Call	P.	Take increased order
	S.	Offer other services/products/promotions
7. Research Call	P.	Define precise information required
	S.	Research for names/contacts etc
8. Qualify an Account Call	P.	Gain specific information.
	S.	Sell interest and confidence in your company.

TELEPHONE INTERVIEW SCREENING FORM

TEAM:	DATE
First NAME:	Surname
ADDRESS:	

Children Age			
Under 16 YRS			

How did you hear of this vacancy ?

PREVIOUS TELEPHONE SELLING EXPERIENCE

ARE YOU WORKING AT PRESENT ?

EMPLOYER

WHERE

DUTIES

SALARY

HOW LONG THERE

WHY ARE YOU
THINKING OF LEAVING

IF ACCEPTABLE
I SHOULD LIKE YOU TO COME FOR AN INTERVIEW. MAY I
SUGGEST

DATE   TIME

PLACE

I WILL SEND YOU AN APPLICATION FOR. WOULD
YOU PLEASE COMPLETE IT AND BRING IT WITH
YOU. THANK YOU FOR RINGING AND I LOOK
FORWARD TO MEETING YOU.

(CHECK FULL ADDRESS)

TELEPHONE SALES CLERK TELEPHONE SCREENING FORM

PHONE HOME				
PHONE WORK				
AGE:	MARITAL STATUS:			

	EXCELLENT	GOOD	FAIR	POOR
FIRST IMPRESSIONS (ASSESS WHEN TALKING)				
Clarity/ Voice				
Bounce				
Enthusiasm				
Confidence				
Persuasiveness				
Warmth				
Totals				

Previous Employment

Employer

Where:

Duties:

Salary:

How long there

If unacceptable
THANK APPLICANT FOR HIS/HER INTEREST AND
PROMISE TO SEND A LETTER TO INFORM HIM/HER
OF YOUR DECISION

SCREENED BY:

INTERVIEW ASSESSMENT SHEET

Qualities	Applicants					
	1	**2**	**3**	**4**	**5**	**6**
General appearance						
Punctuality						
Listening Ability						
Questioning Ability (Job Related)						
Dialogue Skill						
Attitude to job						
Personality						
Attentiveness						
Test Question Response						
Team Blend						
Maturity						
Job Related Experience						
Telephone Manner (Screening & Interview)						
Availability						
Ambitions						
Totals						

1	**Applicants Names**
2	
3	
4	
5	
6	

Scoring Rates	
Poor	1
Average	2
Good	3
Excellent	4

MONITORING FORM FOR TELEPHONE ACCOMPANIMENT (A)

NAME: DATE: NO. OF CALLS MONITORED

VG (VERY GOOD) G (GOOD) S (SATISFACTORY) NI (NEEDS IMPROVEMENT)

BOXES MARKED X AS APPRAISED		VG	G	S	NI	COMMENTS
Product Knowledge	Own Company					
Company Knowledge						
SELLING TECHNIQUES	PREPARATION					
	OPENING THE CALL					
	PRESENTATION					
	OBJECTION HANDLING					
	CLOSING THE SALE					
	CLOSING THE INTERVIEW					
	POSITIVE PHRASES					
	ABILITY TO RANGE SELL					
	SUGGESTED QUANTITIES					
	VOICE NOISES					
	MULTIPLE PROMOTIONS					
COMPETITION	KNOWLEDGE OF PRODUCT					
	REPORTING BACK					
ADMINISTRATION	WORK ORGANISATION					
	ACCURATE DOCUMENTATION					
	CUSTOMER RECORD CARDS					
CUSTOMER	KNOWLEDGE					

GENERAL COMMENTS

ACTION PLAN AGREED

APPRAISED BY	TELEPHONE SALES OPERATOR'S SIGNATURE
NEXT TRAINING PERIOD	
(DATE AND TIME)	

MONITORING FORM FOR TELEPHONE ACCOMPANIMENT (B)

Techniques   Disciplines or Stages of Call

	1. Preparation	2. Opening the Call	3. Order Handling	4. Selling Up	5. Achieving Objectives	6. Ending the Call
Customer/Caller Knowledge						
Objection Handling						
Understanding Emotions/Mood						
Personalising the Call						
Voice & Personality Projection						
Questioning						
Developing Customer Relations						
Recognising and Building Sales Opportunities						
Building the Order						
Positive Benefit Selling						
Product Knowledge						
Closing the Call						

Calls Accompanied	In		Time Start	
Post-Call Administration	Out		Time Finish	

MONITORING FORM FOR TELEPHONE ACCOMPANIMENT (C)

1. Name & Location

Name:	
Location:	

2. Dates

Day & Date:	
Date of last training:	

3. Previous Training Objectives

1.	
2.	
3.	

4. Next Training Objectives

1.	
2.	
3.	

5. Disciplines

Disciplines	Summary Techniques	Rating
Preparation		
Opening the Call		
Handling the order		
Selling Up		
Achieving Objectives		
Ending the Call		
Post-Call Administration		

6. Comments

7. Time

Time Spent . . . . . . Hours	
Call Times	
In Out	

8. Initials

Trainer	
Trainee	
Date of Next Training	

TELESALES DAILY CALL SUMMARY

SITE _____ ZONE _____ NAME _____

DAY/DATE _____

OUTGOING CALLS

CALL No.	CALL TIME	CUSTOMER	D/M	R/B	N/R	ORDER B/C	ORDER D	HIGHLIGHT	COMMENTS

TOTAL CALLS MADE [ ]   RATIO % [ ]

INCOMING CALLS

NAME	TIME	ORDER B/C	ORDER D	HIGHLIGHT	DEL	A/C	OTHER	COMMENTS

TOTAL CALLS RECEIVED [ ]   TOTAL QUERIES [ ]

218

TELEMARKETING PLANNING QUESTIONNAIRE

Company Profile
1. How do you get your sales now?
2. How many salespeople do you have?
   Inside? .... Outside? ....
3. How many customers do you have?
4. What is your market potential?
5. How well-known is your company?
6. What is an average customer worth in terms of sales?
7. What is you annual sales revenue?
8. What do you like about the way your sales are going?
9. What would you like to change or improve?

Product Profile
10. What product/service do you sell?
11. What is your best seller?
12. What would you like to sell more of?
13. What is the major benefit of your product/service?
14. List other features and benefits that really count.
15. How does your pricing compare to your competition?
16. What is your delivery time?
17. Why should your customer buy from you?
18. What markets are you selling to currently?
    Local? .... Regional? .... National? ....
19. What markets would you like to penetrate further?
20. Can you produce a profile of your typical or good customer?
21. What qualification data would you like to have regarding your prospects?
22. What are the major needs of your prospects?
23. On what basis do they mostly make their decision?
    Price ☐ Quality ☐ Service ☐ Delivery ☐
24. What prospect lists or directories do you use?
25. Who is the initial contact?
26. Who is the major decision-maker?

Marketing Profile
28. Do you have a marketing plan?
29. Have you ever used an outside marketing firm? If yes, what were the results of their work?
30. What marketing intelligence would be valuable to your company?
31. What other marketing do you do?
    ☐ Price ☐ Advertising ☐ Direct Mail ☐ Trade shows ☐ Other
32. Could telemarketing enhance those programmes?
33. What sort of literature do your prospects receive about your company?
34. What would you expect to accomplish with telemarketing?
35. What other assistance would you like?
    ☐ Sales ☐ Training ☐ Computerisation ☐ Telephone
36. What would you need to see, hear and feel to know that your programmes were successful?

AUTOMATION PLANNING QUESTIONNAIRE

What are your principal objectives in introducing a sales and marketing automative solution?

Firstly, what type of company are you ....

Would you please circle the most appropriate answer:
(0) Not important   (1) Nice to have   (2) Important   (3) Essential

Reduce administrative burden	0	1	2	3
Reduce staffing levels	0	1	2	3
Increase efficiency of marketing activities	0	1	2	3
Handle larger volumes of marketing activities	0	1	2	3
Cut down response times	0	1	2	3
Improve sales staff communications (internal)	0	1	2	3
Improve customer/prospect communications (external)	0	1	2	3
Improve order hit rate	0	1	2	3
Integrate with existing computer systems	0	1	2	3
Integrate with future computer systems	0	1	2	3

Computer System Users, please indicate how many staff will be using the proposed system
internally:

Marketing	Administration staff ____
Support	Accounts ____
Telesales	Telemarketing ____
Sales	Management ____
Other (please specify)	

externally:

Marketing	Administration staff ____
Support	Accounts ____
Telesales	Telemarketing ____
Sales	Management ____
Other (please specify)	

Sales tracking

	0	1	2	3
Track sales prospects/forecasting	0	1	2	3
Monitor sales activities	0	1	2	3
Prompt next/future contact	0	1	2	3
Account management	0	1	2	3
System generated	0	1	2	3
Prompt next/future contact	0	1	2	3
Enquiry source	0	1	2	3
Lead tracking	0	1	2	3
Call back prompt	0	1	2	3

Correspondence

	0	1	2	3
Automatic mailshots	0	1	2	3
Merge lists	0	1	2	3
Prepare quotations	0	1	2	3
Send standard letters	0	1	2	3
Send individual letters	0	1	2	3
Export database records	0	1	2	3
Import database records	0	1	2	3

Management Information

	0	1	2	3
Sales to date summary	0	1	2	3
Prospects to date summary	0	1	2	3
Activity log	0	1	2	3
User definable reports	0	1	2	3

Contact Database

	0	1	2	3
Customer contacts	0	1	2	3
Contact history	0	1	2	3
Supplier contacts	0	1	2	3
Hotline/Customer satisfaction	0	1	2	3
Purchasing history	0	1	2	3
Enquiry search routines	0	1	2	3
User definable search categories	0	1	2	3
Eliminate record duplication	0	1	2	3

Communications

	0	1	2	3
Internal 'E' mail	0	1	2	3
External 'E' mail	0	1	2	3
Autodial	0	1	2	3
Powerdial	0	1	2	3
Auto fax	0	1	2	3
Remote capability	0	1	2	3
Download to laptop	0	1	2	3

Diary/Task management

	0	1	2	3
Personal calendar	0	1	2	3
Sales staff calendar	0	1	2	3
Personal 'to do' lists	0	1	2	3
Departmental 'to do' lists	0	1	2	3

SAMPLE JOB DESCRIPTION – TELESALES OPERATOR/AGENT

Job Title: Telesales Operator

Responsible To: Telesales Supervisor/Team Leader

Purpose of Job: To achieve agreed sales and promotional targets within own accounts as directed by team leader and in accordance with company policies.

Key Areas:

1. Selling
2. Customer Support
3. Key Account Manager Support
4. Administration
5. Communication
6. Attitude
7. Self-development

1. Selling

- Sell to all accounts designated by team leader and achieve sales volume targets
- Use a structured sales sequence on all outgoing calls
- Sell in new products and promotions and achieve designated targets
- Be conversant with and implement the activity contained in the current month's Telesales Plan

2. Customer Support

- Ensure that all planned outgoing calls are made at the correct time on a daily basis as agreed with the customers
- Handle incoming calls as allocated by team leader quickly and efficiently
- Act promptly with customer queries and ensure follow-up where necessary, do not direct to other departments unless absolutely necessary, you must personally handle all customer queries
- Develop good relationships with own customers in order to ensure confidence in our products and services
- When necessary, cover other calls as designated by Team Leader.

3. Key Account Manager (KAM) Support

- Action and reply to any KAM memorandum or request
- Supply target volume figures to your KAM
- Keep a comprehensive list of all messages for your KAM
- Amend KAM home address label on the computer as and when changes occur
- Process your KAM's catalogue and samples order and monitor progress through the warehouse to ensure availability for collection, and collate stationery requested for collection on the same day
- Distribute customer order history prints

4. Administration

- Complete the weekly report on a daily basis after each call in an accurate and legible manner
- Supply, where necessary, meaningful daily reports to KAMs concerning customers' problems and nil orders
- Keep all customer records and call plans up-to-date and inform Team Leader of all amendments to call plans
- Ensure all your orders are processed through the computer the same day of receipt
- Handle all aspects of incoming and outgoing post
- Handle all aspects of customer's back-order system
- Update and amend customer discounts where applicable

5. Communication

- Ensure Team Leader is kept up-to-date on all outstanding customer queries and problems
- Be prepared to discuss briefly individual customer problems with your KAM when he/she contacts telesales by telephone. Use your KAM's visits to telesales to discuss and solve problems and develop good working relationships with your KAM
- To liaise effectively with all colleagues, managers and directors as and when required
- Have an understanding of other departments' functions and their relation to the telesales department
- Ensure all correspondence to customers is handled quickly and efficiently and includes all relevant information.

6. Attitude

- Project an efficient and professional attitude and be polite and respectful at all times to customers and colleagues
- Do not get involved in personal conversation or interrupt or distract other colleagues during working hours
- Be prepared to be flexible at lunchtimes and start and finish times, when taking customers orders, and always arrive at specified time agreed
- Appearance always to be smart and businesslike

7. Self Development

- To continually analyse own performance and seek improvement
- Obtain a working knowledge of company product range
- Attend training courses and meetings as directed
- Regularly review personal organisation
- Accompany KAM or Team Leader on customer visits as agreed and where appropriate

Annex D
Case Studies

RAC CASE STUDY

The RAC is synonymous with motor vehicle rescue and recovery, but an equally important part of its business is derived from the numerous extra services it offers within its Membership Marketing Division; services such as travel bookings, travel insurance, traffic information, legal and technical advice, new membership enquiries, membership renewals, vehicle inspection and so on. In fact, outside of its roadside rescue business, the RAC offers a broad portfolio of motorist-related products and services to members and non-members.

The bulk of RAC membership-services business is conducted over the telephone from three call centres nationwide. These are based in Bristol, Manchester and Croydon, with the Bristol 'SuperCentre' established just two years ago. In order to provide service across a wide product range and member enquiries, the agents are currently structured in teams, each trained to deal with different parts of the business. This means that, for instance, an existing member wishing to make a travel booking, will call the travel booking telephone number, which is automatically routed to one of the team of agents trained to deal with this particular enquiry. Similarly, a prospective customer requesting a quote for membership will dial a different telephone number and so be routed to a different team.

RAC's strategy is to make their business very accessible to members and motorists and to deliver a one-stop-shop approach for a high proportion of callers, irrespective of the nature of the call. This calls for a large investment not only in front-end technology but also database management and, most importantly, in human resource. An overhaul of its technology was required to achieve these objectives, whilst at the same time protecting the significant investment already made. With the tremendous volumes of telephone calls being made and received across all three sites, which average around 100 000 a week, RAC already had in place an extensive voice and data network. Incoming calls are managed at each site through an Ericsson ACP1000 automatic call distributor with high volume outbound traffic being automated and driven by an EIS predictive dialler.

A change from the mainframe-based data capture environment to the more flexible call centre environment driven by customer calls and delivered through client/server architecture was required. The existing database was transferred onto Oracle which allowed RAC to develop the future growth of client contact and prospecting databases. In doing this, they established a core infrastructure which would endure subsequent change at the front end with relative ease.

Choosing the Co-Cam solution combining BROCK software and Co-Cam's own product, the Co-Cam Call Centre, functions for campaign management, agent management, customer profiling, inbound and outbound call management and customer contact management were all included. PC-based scripting and prompts for agents, tailored to suit each different call type enables more use of the customer database, with breakdown of call type, outcome of call, customer history and improved segmentation. Another important part of the software in place will enable the RAC to capture any prospective enquiry received, such as membership quotes which were not fulfilled.

With the technology in place acting as the enabler to fulfill the RAC's business objectives, the RAC needed to look at the equally important element of agent empowerment and management. For any call centre supervisor this is a crucial role, and in the RAC's case, where the intention in the end of the pilot is to have an operation full of multi-skilled agents, the challenge is enormous. The move from teams of agents skilled in specific areas to the creation of a multi-skilled, single agent team will not happen overnight. Agents are being phased in to the Enterprise Team over the period of the pilot, and will continue to be as the pilot rolls out.

In less than five months, the RAC have implemented the 'new' call centre, a pilot in which RAC has invested more than £1 million. The pilot scheme is already proving a success with staff, has delivered measurably improved business results, and will gradually roll out over the next 18 months. The RAC believes that by the end of 1997 it will truly live up to its 'Supercentre' tag.

HEINZ CASE STUDY

As one of the UK's leading grocery manufacturers, Heinz is committed to providing the most efficient and effective service both to its consumers and its customers. That is why the company is heavily involved in the widely publicised ECR initiative (Efficient Consumer Response), and why it continues to seek new and better ways of configuring every part of its operation, whether it be procurement, production, logistics, trade support, sales or consumer marketing.

One of the primary sales facilitators for Heinz is their telesales team, which handles incoming orders and enquiries from both customers and sales reps in the field by phone and fax.

With millions of orders received every week, represented by several hundred telephone calls, the telesales function at Heinz is business-critical. Quick and easy access to relevant customer and product information is therefore a key requirement to support operators in maximising value at the point of order-capture.

In December 1994, a project was initiated with the core objective to increase productivity through optimum service within the Telesales Business Unit by implementing a system which would facilitate the quick and efficient handling of customer orders and enquiries and support proactive outbound telemarketing activity. Reporting and analysis of both call and order activity was also an essential requirement to support management processes through improved performance measurement.

The MarketForce system chosen currently resides on a Local Area Network at Heinz' offices in Middlesex. Three interfaces have been developed to import customer and product data from the Heinz mainframe corporate database systems into the relevant areas. A fourth interface exports order capture information input by the telesales operators to the mainframe via a batch process, which is run at pre-determined times throughout the day.

Two main databases are at the centre of the telesales operation. A *Direct* customer database, populated from the Heinz mainframe, holds details of customers who deal directly with Heinz, facilitating order capture and allowing the planning and execution of outbound calls. Information relating to customers who do not buy directly from Heinz, but through a wholesaler for example, will be captured in a second *Indirect* customer database for marketing campaigns and analysis.

System security has been set up with different database access rights for the telesales operators, telesales managers and system managers, with applications relevant to each job function.

For the telesales operators, MarketForce supports the work process flow of customer call handling whatever the call type, for example sales rep call, faxed order, customer phone order, general customer enquiry, and so on. Configurable 'panels' within the system have been designed to hold key customer data as required, such as name, address, principal contacts, class of trade, buying group, and so on, as well as a profile of customer products stocked. Additional windows hold unlimited numbers of individual contacts, customer questionnaires for outbound telemarketing surveys and campaigns, and customer specific notes, for example special ordering instructions. The order capture area of the system allows the operator to view standard product pricing and details of current promotional offers, customer ordering history and credit information. The operator can use this information to build the value of the order and then input the order details including delivery dates, times, order numbers, and so on, ready for transference to the Heinz mainframe Sales Order Processing system. If required, the operator can set a date to recall the customer, who will appear in an outbound call list on the specified day.

Outbound calls can also be made to a specified number of existing customers each day and the telesales teams can view all customers due to be called, together with any lapsed or outstanding calls within a single call list, ensuring that no customer is ever 'lost' or forgotten'. The system allows the telesales operators to 'park' an order they are currently entering onto the system and go back to it at a later stage to update/finish, for example, if an inbound phone call is received while inputting a faxed order.

The Telesales Manager has the ability to run either standard or *ad hoc* reports, such as Strike Rate, Order Summary, Inbound/Outbound Call Analysis and Operator Performance as required, and can also design, set up and edit surveys/ questionnaires for the outbound telemarketing team. In addition, the System Manager can access and maintain product and promotional details and manage order deletions.

BASS TAKE-HOME CASE STUDY

Bass Take-Home is the off-trade division of Bass Brewers Limited, and offers an exceptional portfolio of beer brands and the highest levels of customer service.

Since October 1993, Bass Take-Home has operated a customer service/consumer helpline, offering a complete telephone business service to its retail customers and a direct link to Bass for consumers.

An important aspect of the Customer Service operation is the provision of a central Consumer Helpline handling all consumer enquiries regarding product, promotions, pricing and general queries, through a single 'lo-call' helpline number advertised on products. The helpline team of customer services representatives receives up to 600 inbound calls, faxes and letters per day, and follows standard response procedures in order to meet the service levels set out in the Bass Take-Home Charter. The Charter specifies that response to all telephone enquiries must be completed within five hours, and to all written enquiries within five days of receipt.

Bass Take-Home implemented MarketForce sales and marketing software from Market Solutions to provide helpline staff with an efficient means of handling a high volume of incoming enquiries, from initial contact and categorisation through to resolution, in line with service levels. For front-desk users, MarketForce is structured to handle the receipt, categorisation, input and resolution of inbound telephone and written enquiries within the approved Charter levels. The main database holds primary consumer details such as name and address, initially populated from existing Bass systems and external data sources via interfaces. Attached to each consumer record is a profile panel which has been configured to hold additional consumer details for campaign marketing purposes.

The system comprises a multiple database search feature, allowing fast search and retrieval of existing consumer records. Similarly, new consumer details can be quickly captured and validated using PAF functionality. An Enquiry Window, configured to Bass Take-Home's specific needs, allows users to capture details of the enquiry, for example call category, enquiry type, product type, and so on. This information is tied into the Bass Take-Home Charter service levels so that the set response time is automatically logged against the enquiry.

Ease and speed of use is further supported through the use of pop-up data selection tables with further automatic data entry based on the selection made. The window combines a structured set of fields for reporting purposes with unlimited note writing facilities, allowing users to add free text as necessary. On completion of an enquiry, letters can be sent immediately or sent to a queue for batch printing and despatch to fit in with user shift patterns and workflow rate.

Most importantly for front-desk users, Bass required a flexible working environment during peak call times, allowing users to exit an incomplete record whilst taking a new call and then retrieve later for completion. Changes in workflow pattern are also supported, for example when an incoming enquiry requires immediate capture of the enquiry details rather than the caller's name and address, helpline staff can go straight to the Enquiry Window and then complete the consumer's details once the enquiry has been resolved.

Where enquiries cannot be resolved by the front desk (as in approximately 25 per cent of cases), enquiries are escalated to the back desk, using the system's queue handling facility. The back-desk operators can view and sort the queue of 'open' enquiries by priority, date, category or ID, for example, and monitor the involvement of other departments and third parties in actioning calls. A 'traffic light' method is used to monitor enquiries approaching the Bass Take-Home Charter deadlines. For example, enquiries within 2 hours of the deadline are highlighted in green, within one hour in amber, and if beyond the expiry time in red. Thus back-desk users can easily see which enquiries need the most urgent attention and managers can analyse performance against the Charter service levels.

From a management perspective, the system provides extensive and flexible reporting tools, which have been used to set up the required call analysis reports, for example call summary by user, exception report, and so on. Standard reports are added to users' front menus according to their access rights and *ad hoc* reports can be configured as needed, using unlimited search and sort facilities. Full graphical and real time reporting capabilities allow managers to analyse performance at an individual or group level and direct action according to peaks and troughs in volume.

Immediate benefits identified by Bass following the implementation of MarketForce have included the promotion and achievement of better service levels, facilitation of more effective and efficient working practises through effective monitoring of the needs, use and misuse of the helpline, and achievement of all project goals.

Bibliography and Further Information

BIBLIOGRAPHY

Berman, B. (1996) *Marketing Channels* (Canada: John Wiley).

Egan, G. (197) *The Skilled Helper* (Monterey, Calif.: Broos/Cole).

Forsyth, P. (1989) *Running an Effective Sales Office* (Aldershot: Gower).

Hertzberg, F. (1959) *The Motivation to Work* (New York: Wiley).

Holtham, C. (n.d.) "Improving the Performance of Worksgroups through Information Technology," City University Business School.

Jenkinson, A. (1995) *Valuing Your Customers* (Maidenhead: McGraw Hill).

Maslow, A. (1954) *Motivation and Personality* (New York: Harper).

Moriarty, R. T., and Swartz, G. S. (n.d.) "Automation to Boost Sales & Marketing," *Havard Business Review.*

Stevens, M. (1995) *Telemarketing in Action* (Maidenhead: McGraw-Hill).

FURTHER INFORMATION

Call Center Campus

Call Center Campus is an annual three-day conference held at Purdue University and sponsored by Ameritech. Since the emphasis of the program is on call-center assessment and problem solving, participants can expect to receive specific suggestions on how to improve their call centers. In addition, they will obtain three continuing education credits from Purdue University and a personalized evaluation of their call center. The conference is geared toward operations, human resources, technology, internal help desk, and telemarketing managers. For more information contact Dr. Jon Anton by phone at 1-765-494-8357 or by email at DrJonAnton@aol.com.

Call Center Network Group

Through providing programs and services that advance the exchange of ideas, experiences, and solutions, the Call Center Network Group helps call-center professionals meet the challenges of managing a call-center environment. The group also provides opportunities for career advancement, training, and networking across all industries and around the globe. For information on how to become a member, call 1-800-840-2264.

Computer Telephony Expo

This three-day conference and trade show gives call-center professionals an opportunity to sample the latest computer-telephony products and technologies. Through educational conferences, keynotes from industry executives, and full-day tutorials, the expo focuses on emerging trends in the industry. Some of the main areas covered are IP telephony gateways, web-enabled call centers, next generation networks, interactive voice response, communication controllers, customer-centric technologies, open telephony servers, and unified messaging solutions. For more information contact Computer Telephony Expos "http://www.telecomlibrary.com/icons/slug.gif", 12 West 21 Street, New York, NY 10010, or call 1-888-4-CTEXPO.

The Enterprise Computer Telephony Forum

This is an industry organization formed to promote an open, competitive market for computer telephony integration technology. It aims to drive the computer-telephony industry toward an open systems model similar to the computer industry's migration to open systems in the 1980s and 1990s by gaining agreement on multi-vendor implementations of the various international standards for computer telephony needed to enable the entire market to grow. If interested contact Tom Zenisek, president, 303 Park Drive, Foster City, CA 94404.

Impact Learning Systems International

This organization provides call-center–management training programs that focus on the skills needed for the management of a telephone environment. They are designed for managers in customer service, technical support, call centers, help desks, and internal support departments. For more information contact Impact Learning Systems International, P.O. Box 14110, San Luis Obispo, CA 93406 or call 1-800-545-9003.

Other Useful Information

- The Call Center Coach Web Page, www.callcentercoach.com, provides call-center professionals with various resources that deal with the customer relationship management industry.
- Call Center Solutions: 1-800-272-0240
- The ACD Call Center Online Learning Center, www.call-center.net, contains resources, such as a complete article index, reference books, benchmarking studies, vendor yellow pages, and updates on innovative technologies, for call center managers.
- A free subscription to *CallCenter* magazine can be obtained by visiting its web site at www.callcentermagazine.com.
- Computer Telephony Portal, www.computertelephony.org, has over 1,000 categorized computer-telephony links.
- The Lucent Technologies Call Center Institute works with a number of organizations to provide customers with a source for call-center intelligence, knowledge resources, and knowledge-sharing programs. For more information, see www.lucent.com/enterprise/cci/.
- Pacific Call Center Solutions Inc, a call-center consulting firm, can be contacted regarding information on its services at 1164 Bishop Street, #124-417, Honolulu, HI 96813. It can also be reached by phone at 1-808-528-1562 or by email at info@pccsi.com.
- The Resource Center for Customer Service Professionals, www.the-resource-center.com, provides links to books, reports, surveys, self-study training, association memberships, and training seminars from the industry's foremost associations, consulting firms, and publishers.
- The Tele-M@rket for call center, telemarketing and teleservices solutions, www.telemkt.com, presents suppliers with an opportunity to market their products and services to a highly targeted, senior-level audience. It also provides information through online documents, virtual conferences, and discussion forums.

Index

Accounts, 29, 139, 148
ACD, 20, 206–7, 209
Achievement, 100, 107
Advertising, 11, 12, 26, 139, 219
Appraisal, 35, 92–6
Assessment Criteria, 115–17
Attitudes, 56
Auditing, 67–9, 136
Automation, 17, 35, 41, 43, 220–1

Brand Building, 26
Business Plan, 148–9
Business Processes, 18

Call Centre, 48–9, 205–6
Call Objectives, 212
Call Summary, 218
Campaigns, 12, 37
CASM, 51–2
Change, 19, 27, 60, 74–5, 135
Closing, 193–5
CMS, 51
Coaching, 108–11
Collecting Money, 9, 11–12
Communication, 66–7, 130, 173, 177, 223
Company Plan, 4, 7
Competitor Analysis, 170–1
Complaints, 153
Computers, 17
Control, 19, 40
Counselling, 108, 157–8
Cross Selling, 9, 15
CTI, 21, 24, 208–9
Customer Loyalty, 25
Customer Service, 9, 12, 15, 58–60, 71, 206
Data Sources, 34–5
Database, 4, 6, 11, 22, 24, 36–9
Database Marketing, 6

DDI, 21
Debt Collection, 176–8
Delegation, 125–6
Depression, 199–202
Direct Mail Follow Up, 9, 15
Direct Marketing, 6
DMU, 169, 180

Empowerment, 35, 69–70
Environment, 91
Expense, 129

Facilitating, 160
Fear, 62–4, 65, 101–2, 131
Feedback, 35, 159
Field Sales, 40
Follow Through, 150–1
Forecasting, 22, 98
Freephone, 9, 15, 48
Fund Raising, 9

Gaining Appointments, 9, 13
Generating Leads, 8

Handling Objections, 188–93
Homeworking, 173

Image, 152, 167
Incentive, 98–9
Induction, 114
Intangible, 149, 166
Integration, 21, 27, 60, 205
Interview, 95–6, 213, 214
Investment, 15
ISDN, 20
ISM, 52
ISO 9000, 203–5
IVR, 22, 207–8, 209

Loyalty Schemes, 34

Mailing List Testing, 9
Mailing Preference Service, 164
Major Account Management, 29
Management, 29, 34–5, 41, 49, 51–2, 54–5,
    61–6, 76–9, 91, 107, 128–9, 140, 204,
    206
Market Intelligence, 11
Marketing, 4–8, 14, 17–19, 27–8, 34, 41,
    47–8, 130, 148–9, 219
Maslow, 102
Meetings, 120–3
Mentoring, 129
Monitoring, 36, 55, 78, 215, 216, 217
Motivation, 70, 101–8
Multi User Networks, 19

Negotiation, 196
Network, 209
New Product Launch, 14
NVQ, 129–30

Outsourced, 23

Pareto, 165–6
Partnership, 28–9
Performance Standards, 78, 90–2
PIM, 51
Praise, 107
Priorities, 156
Proactive, 57, 124, 157
Procedures, 145–8
Product Life-Cycle, 39–40
Production, 5
Productivity, 17, 71
Project, 54–5
Psychological Testing, 90

Qualifying Prospects, 10–11
Quality, 38, 76–9, 91, 181

Quotations, 9, 13

Reactive, 124–5, 160
Recognition, 100, 107
Recruiting, 12, 80–1
Recruitment, 9
Relationship Marketing, 27
Research, 10, 36, 74, 179, 211, 212
Role, 101

Sales Order Processing, 201
Screening Form, 213
Scripts, 23, 172–3
Selling, 5, 9, 15, 28, 96, 122, 140, 179–80,
    182–3, 186–7, 191
Special Promotions, 12
Strategy, 4–6, 58–60, 103
Stress, 199–202
Substitution, 9
Supervisor, 110, 113
Support, 9, 13, 222
Surveying/Researching, 9, 10
Surveys, 10, 55
SWOT, 55

Targeting, 96–8
Tasks, 69, 111
Team, 22, 27, 29, 60, 68
Telebusiness, 3–4, 56–7, 81, 101, 130–1,
    152
Telephone Etiquette, 152–6
Telesales, 47, 119, 179, 222–3
Test Marketing, 9, 14
Time Management, 123
TQM, 76–9
Training, 61–3, 80, 93, 105, 108–11, 112–
    13, 114, 118, 121, 129–30
Training Schemes, 129–30
Trends, 91

Written Communication, 173